European Computer Driving Licence®

ECDL Advanced

Syllabus 2.0

Module AM3 - Word Processing

Using Microsoft® Word 2007

Release ECDL225v3

Published by:

CiA Training Ltd
Business & Innovation Centre
Sunderland Enterprise Park
Sunderland SR5 2TA
United Kingdom

Tel: +44 (0) 191 549 5002
Fax: +44 (0) 191 549 9005

E-mail: info@ciatraining.co.uk
Web: www.ciatraining.co.uk

ISBN-13: 978 1 86005 650 5

Important Note

This guide was written using *Windows Vista*. If using *Windows XP* some dialog boxes will look different, although the content is the same.

A screen resolution of 1024 x 768 was used. Working in a different screen resolution, or with an application window which is not maximised, will change the look of the *Office 2007* Ribbon. The ribbon appearance is dynamic, it changes to fit the space available. The full ribbon may show a group containing several options, but if space is restricted it may show a single button that you need to click to see the same options, e.g.

the **Editing** group [Editing] may be replaced by the **Editing** button.

This training, which has been approved by ECDL Foundation, includes exercise items intended to assist Candidates in their training for an ECDL Certification Programme. These exercises are not ECDL Foundation certification tests. For information about authorised Test Centres in different national territories, please refer to the ECDL Foundation website at www.ecdl.org

First published 2009

European Computer Driving Licence, ECDL, International Computer Driving Licence, ICDL, e-Citizen and related logos are all registered Trade Marks of The European Computer Driving Licence Foundation Limited ("ECDL Foundation").

CiA Training Ltd is an entity independent of ECDL Foundation and is not associated with ECDL Foundation in any manner. This courseware may be used to assist candidates to prepare for the ECDL Foundation Certification Programme as titled on the courseware. Neither ECDL Foundation nor **CiA Training Ltd** warrants that the use of this courseware publication will ensure passing of the tests for that ECDL Foundation Certification Programme. This courseware publication has been independently reviewed and approved by ECDL Foundation as covering the learning objectives for the ECDL Foundation Certification Programme.

Confirmation of this approval can be obtained by reviewing the Partners Page in the About Us Section of the website www.ecdl.org

The material contained in this courseware publication has not been reviewed for technical accuracy and does not guarantee that candidates will pass the test for the ECDL Foundation Certification Programme. Any and all assessment items and/or performance-based exercises contained in this courseware relate solely to this publication and do not constitute or imply certification by ECDL Foundation in respect of the ECDL Foundation Certification Programme or any other ECDL Foundation test. Irrespective of how the material contained in this courseware is deployed, for example in a learning management system (LMS) or a customised interface, nothing should suggest to the candidate that this material constitutes certification or can lead to certification through any other process than official ECDL Foundation certification testing.

For details on sitting a test for an ECDL Foundation certification programme, please contact your country's designated National Licensee or visit the ECDL Foundation's website at www.ecdl.org.

Candidates using this courseware must be registered with the National Operator before undertaking a test for an ECDL Foundation Certification Programme. Without a valid registration, the test(s) cannot be undertaken and no certificate, nor any other form of recognition, can be given to a candidate. Registration should be undertaken with your country's designated National Licensee at an Approved Test Centre.

Downloading the Data Files

The data associated with these exercises must be downloaded from our website. Go to: *www.ciatraining.co.uk/data*. Follow the on screen instructions to download the appropriate data files.

By default, the data files will be downloaded to **Documents\CIA DATA FILES\Advanced ECDL\AM3 Word 2007 Data**. (Note: *Windows XP* downloads to a **My Documents** folder).

If you prefer, the data can be supplied on CD at an additional cost. Contact the Sales team at *info@ciatraining.co.uk*.

Aims

To demonstrate the ability to use a word processing application on a personal computer.

To understand and accomplish more advanced operations associated with the editing, layout and organisation of a word processed document and the use of various elements and special tools.

To demonstrate some of the more advanced features, including creating master documents, referencing, working with templates, styles, tables, forms, linking and embedding, editing mail merge documents, creating macros and using automatic formatting.

Objectives

After completing the guide the user will be able to:

- Apply advanced text, paragraph, column and table formatting. Convert text to a table and vice versa.

- Work with referencing features like footnotes, endnotes and captions. Create tables of contents, indexes and cross references.

- Enhance productivity by using fields, forms and templates.

- Apply advanced mail merge techniques and work with automation features like macros.

- Use linking and embedding features to integrate data.

- Collaborate on and review documents. Work with master documents and subdocuments. Apply document security features.

- Work with watermarks, sections and headers and footers in a document.

Assessment of Knowledge

At the end of this guide is a section called the **Record of Achievement Matrix**. Before the guide is started it is recommended that the user completes the matrix to measure the level of current knowledge.

Tick boxes are provided for each feature. **1** is for no knowledge, **2** some knowledge and **3** is for competent.

After working through a section, complete the matrix for that section and only when competent in all areas move on to the next section.

Contents

Section 1
Working Efficiently

By the end of this Section you should be able to:

Appreciate Design Considerations

Recognise Different Techniques That Are Available

Create and Use Hyperlinks

Save Documents in Various Formats

To gain an understanding of the above features, work through the **Driving Lessons** in this **Section**.

For each **Driving Lesson**, read the **Park and Read** instructions, without touching the keyboard, then work through the numbered steps of the **Manoeuvres** on the computer. Complete the **Revision Exercise(s)** at the end of the section to test your knowledge.

Driving Lesson 1 - Design

Park and Read

Whilst any course on advanced word processing applications needs to describe and explain the techniques necessary to produce successful documents, thought should always be given to overall purpose of the finished document and to the intended target audience.

Purpose

Every document produced has a purpose. Before starting to create a document, take some time to consider the purpose behind it and plan the content and style accordingly.

Example 1. Assume you are creating a CV. Its purpose is to communicate to a potential employer the relevant features of your qualifications and experience in an easily accessible format. The style may vary depending on the type of job involved, but the content is almost predetermined. Because of the purpose, the information will probably be summarised and presented in list or table form rather than in a rambling free-form letter.

Example 2. You are creating a poster to advertise a future event for your club or society. Its purpose will be to catch people's eye and to communicate key details of the event, such as content, location and date. So make sure your document is both eye catching and includes all relevant details accurately.

Example 3. You are writing documentation for a new IT system. You must know the purpose of the documentation before starting it. Is it to guide users through its operation, or is it to describe the technical specification so that IT staff can maintain it? Each purpose would result in a completely different document.

Audience

The intended audience can have a major impact on both the content and style of the final document, e.g. a report on company performance may be different if intended for the general staff, or for the Financial Director, and a letter to a friend would look different to a business letter to a customer.

With technical content you should also be aware of the level of knowledge the audience has of the subject and plan the document accordingly. Too much explanation of areas with which the audience is familiar may cause them to lose interest. Likewise, too little explanation for an audience with little or no subject knowledge may have the same effect.

Data sources

Word allows complex documents to contain information drawn from a wide variety of sources, e.g. embedded spreadsheets and charts, database tables as merge sources, images from libraries. When planning your document, make sure you consider the availability and accuracy of all such sources.

Driving Lesson 1 - Continued

Other Considerations

The final form of your document may also affect its style. A printed report may reasonably contain a large amount of detail, possibly divided with headings and subheadings. If the same data is to become the content for a web page or presentation, it would probably need to be more summarised, with more bullet points and visual content.

There may also be other practical considerations to take into account. You might be asked to produce a one page summary or a 1000 word report. Such restrictions would obviously have a major effect on your document plan.

 Manoeuvres

1. Look at the two warning notices below. The road safety poster is aimed at children, the entry regulations are for trained technical staff.

2. Consider the purpose and audience for the two notices and how these factors have affected the style and content.

3. Think how effective the posters would be if the styles were reversed.

Driving Lesson 2 - Techniques

▣ Park and Read

Word processing software such as *Microsoft Word* enables you to produce professional looking, well styled documents for many different purposes. No matter what type of job you do, it's likely that at some stage you'll need to create a document, e.g. a business letter, an invoice, a newsletter, a report.

In particular, *Word* has many features that allow you to create complex documents, i.e. multi page documents containing a variety of formatting styles and techniques, and possibly containing or referencing content originally from different applications. Some of the relevant skills and techniques are:

- **Hyperlinks**. Links to allow users of the documentation to access relevant data from other sources.

- **Advanced text and paragraph editing**. Including text wrap, text orientation, paragraph spacing and the use of styles.

- **Templates**. Allowing many documents to be based on the same consistent look.

- **Collaborative editing**. Including tracking of changes and working with comments.

- **Document layout techniques**. Including the use of sections and multiple columns.

- **Referencing techniques**. Such as the creation of tables of contents, indexes, footnotes, endnotes and captions.

- **Master documents**. Creating multi-chapter documents using master documents and sub-documents.

- **Field codes**. Substituting current data into documents using field codes.

- **Forms**. Allow user entered data into a document using forms and form fields.

- **Tables**. Present and manipulate data in a document using tables.

- **Mail merge**. Including the editing of data source tables.

- **Macros**. Instructions to perform repetitive tasks with a single command.

Driving Lesson 3 - Hyperlinks

▣ Park and Read

When a document is being viewed on screen, there are ways of making it easier for users to move to different locations within the document or to access connected information held in other locations. This is done using **hyperlinks**. A hyperlink can be applied to any piece of text or object in a document so that clicking the object will display another location in the document, which has been defined with a bookmark. Alternatively the hyperlink may open a different file, a web page, or your e-mail application. Some features, such as **Table of Contents**, use hyperlinks automatically.

↱ Manoeuvres

1. Open the supplied data file **Links**. This is a multi-page document that has had a table of contents created.

2. On the first page, hold down the **<Ctrl>** key and move the mouse pointer over the first line of the table of contents. Because this is a hyperlink, the cursor changes to a pointing hand.

3. With the **<Ctrl>** key still held down, click the mouse button. Page 2 of the document is displayed.

4. Scroll back to the first page and highlight the title, **Contents.** Select the **Insert** tab and click on **Bookmark** from the **Links** group.

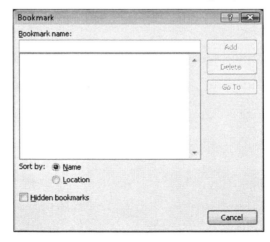

5. Enter **Contents** as the **Bookmark name** and click the **Add** button.

Driving Lesson 3 - Continued

6. Move to the last sentence of the <u>last page</u> of the document, highlight the word **here**, and click **Hyperlink**, [Hyperlink].

7. Make sure **Place in This Document** is selected from the left of the dialog box, and if necessary click the ⊞ at the left of **Bookmarks** to reveal the list of available bookmarks.

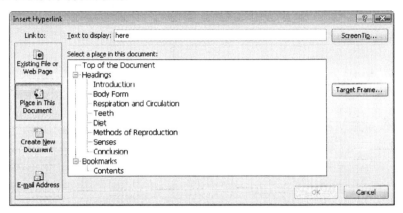

ℹ️ *By default you can hyperlink to headings and the top of the document.*

8. Select **Contents** and click **OK**. The hyperlink is applied.

9. Click on the word **here** with the **<Ctrl>** key held down to move to the **Contents** bookmark.

10. Move to page 2 and click to select the **shark** image. Click [Hyperlink] and select **Existing File or Web Page**.

11. You can browse to locate any file or web page on your system to be the target of your hyperlink, or you can type a value into **Address**. For this exercise type **www.ciatraining.co.uk** and click **OK** to insert the hyperlink.

12. Click anywhere on the **shark** image with the **<Ctrl>** key held down to open the **CiA Training** web page (if you have an live Internet connection).

13. Close your browser, and click on the **shark** image to select it. Existing hyperlinks can be amended.

14. Click [Hyperlink]. The **Edit Hyperlink** dialog box is displayed. Change the **Address** to **www.ciasupport.co.uk** and click **OK**.

15. Test the link then close the browser.

16. Right click on the shark image (or any other hyperlink text) and select **Remove Link**. The hyperlink is removed.

17. Close the **Links** document <u>without</u> saving.

Driving Lesson 4 - Saving

▣ Park and Read

Although the usual format for saving documents is as a **Word Document** (with a **.doc** extension), it is possible to save them in many different formats. One file type is **Plain Text** (with a **.txt** file extension). This means that all formatting, styles and graphics are removed, reducing the file to the simplest text format, making it much smaller and recognisable by most other applications. To save in a format that can be read by any version of *Word*, but still keeps some of the original formatting, save in **Rich Text Format** (**.rtf** file extension). To enable a document to be viewed as a web page, it can be saved in **.htm** format. The location of saved files can also be specified.

↱ Manoeuvres

1. Open the supplied data file **Links2**. This is a multi page document that has had a table of contents and hyperlinks created.

2. Select the **Office Button**, ⬤ and then **Save As**.

3. Select a different save location, i.e. not the original folder for the file. Use the **Create New Folder** button, 🖿, to create a new folder if you wish. Make a note of the new location.

4. Change the **File name** to **Links3**.

5. Click the drop down arrow from the **Save as type** box and view the various options and their file name extensions. Select **Plain Text (*.txt)**.

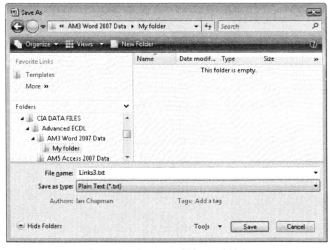

Saving the File to a new folder (My folder)

Driving Lesson 4 - Continued

6.   Click **Save**. If a dialog box appears warning about loss of formatting, click **OK**.

7.   Select **Save As** again and keep the same location.

8.   Change the **File name** to **Links4**, select **Rich Text Format (*.rtf)** and click **Save**.

9.   Select **Save as** again and keep the same location.

10.   Change the **File name** to **Links5** and change **Save as type** to **Web Page (*.htm, *.html)**.

11.   Click **Save**.

12.   Close any open documents.

13.   Minimize *Word* and use the **Documents** window to view the contents of the folder used to save the files **Links3**, **Links4** and **Links5** above.

14.   Double click on **Links3.txt** to open it. If you need to specify an application, choose *Notepad*. The text content is all present, but virtually no formatting and no special features such as images or links have been retained. Close the application.

15.   Double click on **Links4.rtf** to open it. If you need to specify an application, choose *Word*. Notice that the content, formatting and features have all been retained.

16.   Close the document.

17.   Minimize *Word*. Double click on **Links5.htm** to open it. It should open in your default web browser application, e.g. *Microsoft Internet Explorer*. The content is all present, and most of the formatting is retained even though the web page may look a little different.

18.   All hyperlinks now work by simple clicking, it is not necessary to hold down the <**Ctrl**> key. Test their operation.

19.   Close the browser.

20.   Close the window showing the new folder.

Driving Lesson 5 - Revision: Working Efficiently

This is not an ECDL test. Testing may only be carried out through certified ECDL test centres. This covers the features introduced in this section. Try not to refer to the preceding Driving Lessons while completing it.

1.   When designing a document, which 2 main factors should be taken into consideration?

2.   What types of objects from other software applications can be included in a *Word* document?

3.   What is the name for a document that is made up of separate, subdocuments?

4.   What feature allows many different documents to be based on the same, consistent look?

5.   What feature allows users to move to different locations within a document, or to a different location?

6.   Which is the simplest format that a text document can be saved in?

7.   Which format allows you to save a document in a format that can be viewed on the Internet?

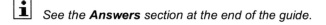 See the **Answers** section at the end of the guide.

If you experienced any difficulty completing this Revision refer back to the Driving Lessons in this section. Then redo the Revision.

Once you are confident with the features, complete the Record of Achievement Matrix referring to the section at the end of the guide. Only when competent move on to the next Section.

Section 2
Text Editing

By the end of this Section you should be able to:

Use Advanced Find and Replace Options

Use Paste Special Options

Use AutoCorrect and AutoFormat

Create AutoText

Change Text Flow and Wrap

To gain an understanding of the above features, work through the **Driving Lessons** in this **Section**.

For each **Driving Lesson**, read the **Park and Read** instructions, without touching the keyboard, then work through the numbered steps of the **Manoeuvres** on the computer. Complete the **Revision Exercise(s)** at the end of the section to test your knowledge.

Driving Lesson 6 - Find and Replace

▣ Park and Read

The **Find and Replace** feature allows you to search a document for specific words, phrases and sentences. However, you can also use it to find or replace other items such as page breaks, paragraph marks and specific formatting of fonts and paragraphs.

☞ Manoeuvres

1. Open the document **Aurora Formatted**, making sure the cursor is at the beginning of the document.

2. Specific formatting in the document can be seen using **Show/Hide**, but in this case, to find the paragraph marks, select **Find** from the **Editing** group on the **Home** tab.

3. Click ![More >>] to reveal extra search options.

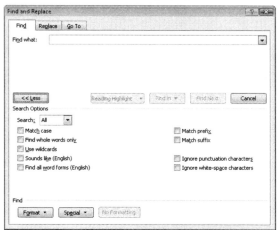

4. Click ![Special ▾] and from the list select **Paragraph Mark**. Notice that **^p** is entered in **Find what**.

5. Click **Find Next** and continue through the document until the following message appears:

Driving Lesson 6 - Continued

6.   Click **OK**.

7.   Click ⌊ Special ▾ ⌋ again and, this time, find where the manual page break has been made.

8.   When you've done this, delete the **^m** entry in **Find what**.

9.   To find the paragraph that has been justified, click ⌊ Format ▾ ⌋ then select **Paragraph**. From **Alignment** select **Justified**.

10. Click **OK** and then **Find Next**. The justified paragraph is highlighted; click **Find Next** again and then **OK** at the message.

11. Click ⌊ Format ▾ ⌋ and select **Paragraph** again and make sure **Alignment** is cleared. Click **OK**.

12. Click ⌊ Format ▾ ⌋ and select **Font**. To find the red text in the document click the drop down list for **Font color** and choose red from **Standard Colors**. Click **OK**.

13. Click **Find Next** to locate the red text. Click **Find Next** again to check for any more red text, then click **OK**.

14. Formatting can also be replaced using the **Replace** feature. Click the **Replace** tab, Place the cursor in the **Replace with** box and click ⌊ Format ▾ ⌋ and then **Font** and from **Font color,** select **Blue**. Click **OK**.

15. Click **Find Next**. Click **Replace** to change the **red** text to **blue**. Continue to Replace until the **Word has finished...** message appears, click **OK**.

16. To remove the search criteria, place the cursor in the **Find what** box, click ⌊ Format ▾ ⌋ and then **Font** and from **Font color** select **Automatic**. Click **OK**. Repeat for the **Replace with** box.

> 📋 *Formatting criteria can be removed quickly by clicking the **No Formatting** button with the cursor in the required box.*

17. Special characters can also be replaced using the **Replace** feature. Click the **Replace** tab.

18. With the cursor in the **Find what** box, click **Special** and select **Manual Page Break**.

19. Click in the **Replace with** box, click **Special** and select **Paragraph Mark**.

20. Click **Find Next**. Click **Replace** to change the page break with a paragraph mark.

> 📋 *A multiple replace is achieved by clicking **Replace All**.*

21. Click **OK** and close the **Find and Replace** dialog box.

22. Close the document <u>without</u> saving.

Driving Lesson 7 - Paste Special Options

▣ Park and Read

Cut and paste is a very useful, time saving feature, but if you simply paste, the text will be added with its original formatting and any styles it contains will automatically be brought into the destination document. **Paste special** gives you more control over how the cut or copied text is added to the document. You can choose whether to paste the text with formatting, or without.

⌐ Manoeuvres

1. Start a new, blank document and at the top enter your name. Press **<Enter>**.

2. Open the document **Stylish** and copy paragraphs 1 and 2 (**Background** and **The House**).

3. Switch back to the new document and click **Paste**.

4. Notice how all the styles have been copied with the text from **Stylish** and pasted into your document. This has created a new page, as the style applied to **Background** has a page break before it.

5. **Undo** the paste action and click the drop down arrow on the **Paste** button. Select **Paste Special**.

6. Select **Unformatted Text** and click **OK**. Notice how the default formatting of the new document has been applied.

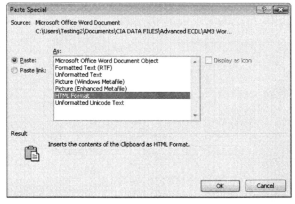

7. Press **<Enter>** and the select **Paste Special**. This time select **Formatted Text (RTF)** and click **OK**. All the styles have been brought in again. However, at the end of the pasted text, notice the **Paste Options Smart Tag**, 🗐. Click on it - even after pasting you can still remove formatting. Select **Match Destination Formatting** and all the original styles are replaced with those from the new document.

8. Close the documents <u>without</u> saving.

Driving Lesson 8 - AutoCorrect

Park and Read

AutoCorrect is a tool that can automatically replace certain text with alternative text as you type. The most widespread use for this is to correct common spelling errors, so that for example "**teh**" can be added so that it changes automatically to "**the**". It is also possible to replace common grammatical errors, and there are options to correct capitalisation mistakes.

Manoeuvres

1. Start a new document and type in the following text, exactly as it appears:

    the ship sailed past the pier and into teh open sea.

2. Notice how spelling and capitalisation errors are automatically corrected. Now type in the days of the week, each followed by a space, but do not capitalise the first letter. This error is also automatically corrected.

3. Click the **Office Button**, then **Word Options**. Make sure **Proofing** is selected at the left and click **AutoCorrect Options...**. Note which capitalisation options are checked. To see which text will be automatically replaced by **AutoCorrect,** scroll down the list of entries.

4. New entries can also be added. In the **Replace** box, enter your initials and in the **With** box, enter your full name. Click on **Add**, then click **OK** and **OK** again.

5. Now type in your initials, press **<Spacebar>** and they are automatically replaced with your full name.

6. Display the **AutoCorrect** dialog box. Scroll through to find your initials. Click on them once, enter a change to the previous entry in the **With** box, click **Replace**, click **Yes** to redefine the entry. Click **OK** and **OK** again.

7. Now type in your initials, press **<Spacebar>** and they are automatically replaced with your redefined name.

8. Display the **AutoCorrect** dialog box again. Scroll through to find your initials. Click on them once and then **Delete** to remove the entry. Click **OK** and click **OK** again to close the **Word Options** dialog box.

9. Close the document <u>without</u> saving.

Driving Lesson 9 - AutoFormat

🅿 Park and Read

Some formatting of documents can be applied automatically, either as text is being entered or afterwards in a separate step. This is called **AutoFormat**. Once a document has been altered in this way, it is still possible to change the formatting.

Manoeuvres

1. Open the document **Papillon**.

2. Display the **AutoCorrect** dialog box as described in the previous driving lesson and select the **AutoFormat** tab to see the features that will be applied when **AutoFormat** is run. Look under the **AutoFormat As You Type** tab to see which options will be applied as you enter text. For this exercise **Built-in Heading styles** should be 'on' in **AutoFormat** and 'off' in **As You Type**.

3. Click **OK** to close the dialog box and then **OK** again. Above the first paragraph, enter the title **Background**, press **<Enter>** to create a paragraph title.

4. In the same way, add the title **Escape** to the second paragraph. Make sure there is a blank line between the first paragraph and the second title.

ℹ️ *AutoFormat is not displayed by default in Word 2007. To add it to the **Quick Access Toolbar**, click the **Office Button**, ⬤, then ⬛ Word Options. Click **Customize** in the **Word Options** dialog box. From the **Choose commands from** list select **All Commands**. From the list of commands in the category, select **AutoFormat**, click **Add**, and then **OK**.*

5. Click the **AutoFormat** button, 🗎 on the **Quick Access Toolbar** to display the **AutoFormat** dialog box.

6. Select **AutoFormat now** and click **OK**. Note the document changes.

7. Print the document and close it <u>without</u> saving.

8. Open **Aurora**.

9. Add the following paragraph titles: **Causes**, **Locations**, **Height** and **Mythology**.

10. **AutoFormat** this document, print it and close it <u>without</u> saving.

Driving Lesson 10 - AutoText

▣ Park and Read

Phrases (or graphics) that are used frequently can be stored in an **AutoText** list, so that they can quickly be added to a document. The required text can be given a different name to identify it and can be called up at any time.

Once an **AutoText** entry has been created, it can be inserted into any document. Some **AutoText** entries already exist within *Word* and can be found within the **Building Blocks Organizer**..

⌐ Manoeuvres

1.   Open the document **Apology**.

ℹ️ *Like **AutoFormat**, **AutoText** can be added to the **Quick Access Toolbar**. Click the **Office Button**, then* 🔲 **Word Options** *. Click **Customize** in the **Word Options** dialog box. In **Choose commands from**, select **Commands Not in the Ribbon**. Scroll down and select **AutoText** then click **Add**. Click **OK**.*

2.   Move to the end of the document and select the text **Customer Care Manager**.

3.   From the **Quick Access Toolbar**, click **AutoText**, . Click **Save Selection to AutoText Gallery** at the bottom of the drop down menu. The **Create New Building Block** dialog box appears.

4.   For the **Name** of the **AutoText entry**, type in **Title**.

☞

Driving Lesson 10 - Continued

5.   Click **OK**. If the name **Title** already exists in the **AutoText** list, the following dialog box appears.

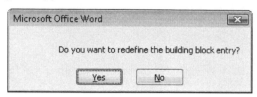

6.   To modify the existing entry, click **Yes**.

7.   After **at your convenience** in the second paragraph, type **The also wishes to visit you**.

8.   Position the cursor between **The** and **also**, then click the **AutoText** button.

9.   **Title**, the entry created earlier, is available from the list in the dropdown menu. Scroll down and click on it to place the **AutoText** in the document. Adjust the spacing if necessary.

10. To delete the **Title AutoText**, click the **AutoText** button, scroll down the list and right click on the **Title** entry.

11. Click **Organize and Delete** and the **Building Blocks Organizer** is displayed, with the **Title AutoText** highlighted. Click **Delete** and then **Yes**. Close the **Organizer**.

12. Close **Apology** without saving and start a new document.

13. Some words, such as days of the week and months, can be inserted automatically. Start to type **Monday** and when the box appears, | Monday (Press ENTER to Insert) / Mond |, press **<Enter>** to complete the entry. This is called **AutoComplete**.

14. Close the document <u>without</u> saving.

Driving Lesson 11 - Text Flow and Wrap

▣ Park and Read

There are a variety of formatting options available when including objects such as graphical objects and tables in text. They can have their own space within the text or they can be included within text blocks so that the text 'wraps' around them. This can be either on one side of the object or the other, or on both sides. Alternatively the object can be placed behind the text.

⌐ Manoeuvres

1. Open the **Wrapping** document.

2. Look at the first image on page 2. This is a **Clip Art** image. It has its own fixed space in the text (this example is in its own paragraph) and the layout is known as **In line with text**. This is the default layout when inserting images.

3. Right click on the image and select **Text Wrapping**. Select **More Layout Options**. The **Wrapping style** is **In line with text**.

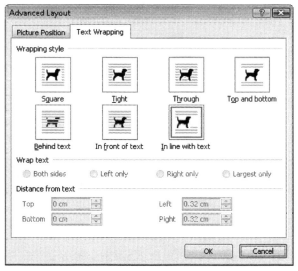

4. Click on the **Square** option for **Wrapping style** and from **Wrap text** select **Left only**. Click **OK**. The image is now 'floating' and the text is wrapped on the left.

5. Drag the image to the right margin and up until it aligns with the top of the first paragraph on the page. As the image is moved, the text is automatically reformatted around it.

Driving Lesson 11 - Continued

6.   Right click on the picture of the tower on this page, and select **Text Wrapping** and the **Square** option. The text is wrapped on both sides of the picture.

7.   Drag the picture to the left margin and align with the top of the last paragraph on the page. The text wraps to the right of the picture.

8.   Right click on the picture below the **Pets Corner** text, and select **Text Wrapping** and **Tight**.

9.   Now the text is wrapped more tightly to the shape of the picture. Drag the picture up until it aligns with the top of the text paragraph.

10. Right click on the **Smiley Face** drawn shape below the **Gift Shop** text, and select **Format Autoshape**, **Layout** tab.

11. Select **Behind text** option for **Wrapping style** and **Center** for **Horizontal alignment**. Click **OK**.

12. The image is now seen behind the text. Drag it up so that it is behind the **Gift Shop** text.

13. Text can be wrapped around other objects. Click in the table in the **Tea Room** text and from the **Layout** tab, click **Properties** in the **Table** group.

14. With the **Table** tab in the dialog box displayed, select an **Alignment** of **Right** and a **Text wrapping** of **Around**.

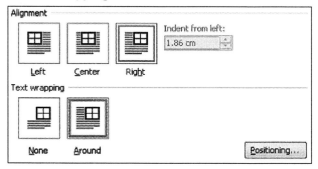

15. Click **OK**.

16. Click on the **Visitor** chart on the last page and click **Position** on the **Format** tab. Select **Position in Top Right with Square Text Wrapping**.

17. Drag the chart down until it aligns with the top of the paragraph text.

18. Click on the organisation chart on the last page and from the **Format** tab select **Arrange**, then **Position**. Select **Position in Middle Left with Square Text Wrapping**.

19. Close the document <u>without</u> saving.

Driving Lesson 12 - Revision: Text Editing

This is not an ECDL test. Testing may only be carried out through certified ECDL test centres. This covers the features introduced in this section. Try not to refer to the preceding Driving Lessons while completing it.

1. Open the document **Birds**.

2. Use the advanced **Find and Replace** options to find **Footnote Marks (Special)**.

> ℹ️ *Make sure the dialog box does not already contain any formatting search criteria, e.g. font colour red, or this will not work.*

3. Find all paragraph marks in the document.

4. On a blank line below the first paragraph, insert the image **branch** from the supplied data.

5. By changing the properties of the picture and moving it, position it so that it appears on the right of the page, aligned with the top of the first paragraph and with the text wrapped around it.

6. Select the picture at the end of the document and change the format so that it appears in the centre of the last paragraph, behind the text.

7. Which method of pasting would you use if you wanted to keep all formatting from the source document?

8. Create an **AutoText** entry, for the text **Created for you by *Your name***.

9. Insert the **AutoText** just created, on a new line at the end of the document.

10. Print the document then delete the **AutoText** entry.

11. Close the document <u>without</u> saving.

> ℹ️ *See the **Answers** section at the end of the guide.*

If you experienced any difficulty completing this Revision refer back to the Driving Lessons in this section. Then redo the Revision.

Once you are confident with the features, complete the Record of Achievement Matrix referring to the section at the end of the guide. Only when competent move on to the next Section.

Section 3
Paragraph Editing

By the end of this Section you should be able to:

Amend Line Spacing

Change Paragraph Pagination Options

Create and Modify Styles

Apply Outline Levels to Styles

Work with Multilevel Lists

To gain an understanding of the above features, work through the **Driving Lessons** in this **Section**.

For each **Driving Lesson**, read the **Park and Read** instructions, without touching the keyboard, then work through the numbered steps of the **Manoeuvres** on the computer. Complete the **Revision Exercise(s)** at the end of the section to test your knowledge.

Driving Lesson 13 - Line Spacing

▣ Park and Read

The amount of space between lines in paragraphs can be changed using the **Paragraph** dialog box. Increasing line spacing can sometimes make paragraphs easier to read. There are various advanced spacing options:

At least   minimum spacing - can be adjusted by *Word* to accommodate larger font sizes that would otherwise not fit the spacing specified.

Exactly   specific, fixed spacing that *Word* does not adjust - makes all lines evenly spaced regardless of font size.

Multiple/proportional   spacing increased or decreased by a user specified amount. **Word 2007** has a default line spacing of **1.15** lines, although this can of course be changed.

☞ Manoeuvres

1. Open the document **Birds** and place the cursor in the first paragraph. This spacing is to be increased proportionally, i.e. doubled.

2. Select the **Paragraph Launcher** and from **Line spacing** select **Multiple**. From **At** enter **2.3**.

    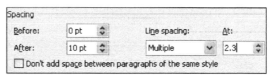

3. Click **OK**.

4. To see what will happen if you reduce this spacing display the **Paragraph** dialog box and type **0.9** in **At**. Click **OK**.

5. Increase the font of this paragraph to **20pt**. Display the dialog box again and from **Line spacing** choose **Exactly** and **12pt**. Click **OK**. Notice that some text has been lost, because the exact spacing is not taking account of the font size.

6. Change the line spacing to **At least 12pt** and notice the difference; *Word* has automatically allowed for the large font.

7. Change the font size back to **10pt**. Change all the paragraph line spacing to **1.5 lines**.

8. Save the document as **Birds2** and close it.

Driving Lesson 14 - Pagination Options

▣ Park and Read

The **Widow/Orphan** control prevents *Word* from separating the last line of a paragraph and printing it at the top of a new page (**widow**), or separating the first line of a new paragraph and leaving it at the bottom of the current page (**orphan**). By default, the control is <u>on</u>.

℞ Manoeuvres

1. Open the document **Widows and orphans**. Scroll down until you can see the bottom of page one and the top of page two on the screen.

2. As the **Widow/Orphan** control is on, the last (or first) line of text from a paragraph is not allowed to be on a page by itself, so two lines of text are kept together at the top of page two.

3. To turn off the control, select the whole document and display the **Paragraph** dialog box by clicking the arrow at the bottom right of the **Paragraph** group. Select the **Line and Page Breaks** tab.

4. From the **Pagination** area, remove the check from the **Widow/Orphan control** box.

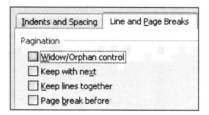

5. Click **OK**. How many lines of text are now left at the top of page two?

6. Turn the control back on by reselecting the **Widow/Orphan control** option. Select the **Keep Lines Together** option, then click **OK**.

7. Observe how with this option selected the whole final paragraph is now kept together by moving it to the second page.

8. Close the document <u>without</u> saving.

ⓘ *See the **Answers** section at the end of the guide.*

Driving Lesson 15 - Creating Styles

P Park and Read

Although there are many formatting styles available by default, it is possible to create others. Styles can be created from scratch or, more usually, they can be based on other styles.

Manoeuvres

1. Open the document **Summary** and add a title **Computer Applications**.

2. Add the following sub headings to the paragraphs:

   Paragraph 1 - **Databases**

   Paragraph 2 - **Word Processing**

   Paragraph 3 - **Spreadsheets**

   Paragraph 4 - **Presentations**

3. Select the main title, then click the **Styles** window launcher on the **Home** tab to display the **Styles** task pane. Click **New Style**, 🔠, to create a new style.

4. In **Name** enter **MainHead**. Make sure **Style type** is **Paragraph** and **Style based on** shows **Normal**.

5. From the **Formatting** area click on the **Font** drop down list and set the **Font** to **Arial** (or similar).

6. In the dialog box, click the **Bold** button, **B**, the **Center** button, ▤, and change the font size to **14**.

7. Click the **Increase Paragraph Spacing** button, 🔲, to increase the spacing before and after the style.

8. Click **OK** to finish creating the style. It is applied to the heading.

Driving Lesson 15 - Continued

9. Click in the first paragraph of text and click again in the **Styles** task pane. Name the style **Text**. Base it on **Normal**.

 Two styles cannot have the same name. Style names can be up to 253 characters long but cannot include \, { } or ;.

10. Ensure the **Font** is **Times New Roman**, **12pt**.

11. Set the **Alignment** to **Justify** and click **Increase Indent**, ⬛, to set the left indent at **1.27cm**. Click **OK**.

 *To customise any of these measurements or settings, click the **Format** button and select an option from the list.*

12. Position the cursor within the second paragraph and choose the **Text** style. Repeat for the remaining paragraphs.

13. Highlight the title **Databases**. Use the **Font** group to format the text as **Arial**, **Bold**, **Italic**, **12 pt**.

14. Click the **New Style** button and type **SubHead** to replace the highlighted entry. Click **OK** to create the style based on the selected text.

15. Format the remaining paragraph headings as **SubHead** by selecting the headings and clicking the **SubHead** entry in the **Styles** window.

16. It is also possible to create **Character** styles which only affect the text itself. Click the **New Style** button and name the style **Red**.

17. Use the **Style type** drop down list and select **Character**.

18. In the **Formatting** section, use the drop down list to select a colour of red, and select the **Underline** option. Click **OK**.

19. Highlight the main heading and click the **Red** style from the list. Highlight the whole second paragraph and select **Red**. Notice that when the **Red** character style is applied, the existing paragraph style is always retained.

20. Save the document as **Applications** and leave it open for the next Driving Lesson.

Driving Lesson 16 - Modifying Styles

🅿 Park and Read

Once styles have been created and applied they can be changed at any time. A change to a style will change all the text in a document to which that style has been applied, ensuring continuity throughout the document.

👉 Manoeuvres

1. With **Applications** still open from the previous exercise, make sure the **Styles** pane is displayed.

2. Click on the drop down arrow at the right of the **SubHead** style and click **Modify** to change the formatting of this style.

3. From the **Modify Style** dialog box, click **Format** then **Font**. Change the **Font style** to **Italic** and check **Small caps** from the **Effects** area.

4. Click **OK**. Click the **Format** button | Format ▾ | and select **Numbering**. From the **Numbering** tab choose the second numbering option. Click **OK** then **OK** again.

5. Notice that all **SubHead** text is updated with the changes.

6. Click on the drop down arrow at the right of the **Red** character style and click **Modify**.

7. Remove the **Underline** formatting and click **OK**. All text that had the **Red** style applied is changed.

8. Save the document and close it.

Driving Lesson 17 - Outline Level Styles

▣ Park and Read

You can assign an **Outline level** paragraph property to styles and then use **Outline View** to show the hierarchy of those styles within a document. By default the styles **Heading 1**, **Heading 2**, have outline levels **1** and **2** respectively, but levels can be assigned to any style.

Within **Outline View**, a document can be collapsed to show only those headings contained within it, or expanded so the entire document can be seen. This view also makes moving around a large document or moving text easier.

Outline level text can be demoted (moved down a level) or promoted (moved up by a level). All of the selected text will then be reformatted accordingly. It is easy to reposition text within a document using **Outline View**. If text formatted as a heading is moved, all text associated with that heading is also moved.

⌐ Manoeuvres

1. Open **Stylish**. The document heading styles are to have outline levels applied, so that the document can be manipulated in **Outline View**.

2. The **Styles** task pane should still be displayed, if not click the dialog box launcher arrow, ▣, at the right of the **Styles** group.

3. In the **Styles** pane, click the arrow at the right of the **TitleHead** style name, and select **Modify**.

4. Select **Format** then **Paragraph** and on the **Indents & Spacing** tab set the **Outline level** to **Level 1**.

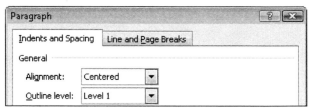

5. Click **OK** and then **OK** again to apply the modification.

6. In a similar way, modify the **MainHead** style as **Level 2** and the **Parahead** style as **Level 3**,

7. Select the **View** tab and click the **Outline** button, to display the **Outlining** tab and the whole document in **Outline** view.

👉

Driving Lesson 17 - Continued

8. On the **Outlining** tab, click the **Show Level** drop down list and select **Level 3**. Only Level **1**, **2** and **3** style text will be displayed.

9. Now select **Level 2** and notice the change.

10. Redisplay **Level 3** and double click on ⊕ next to **The Gardens** to expand that title only.

11. Double click again to collapse the text.

12. Save the changes to the document using the same name and close it.

13. Open the document **Styles** and change to **Outline** view.

14. To move the heading **Equality**, first select the heading and paragraph associated with it, then collapse the text by clicking 🔳 from the **Outline Tools** group.

15. To move the heading and its associated text upwards, position the cursor within the heading and continue to click **Move Up**, 🔳, until the text is above **Background**.

16. To make sure the text has been moved, double click 🔳 to expand the heading.

> ℹ️ *Text can also be moved by positioning the mouse over the ⊕ next to the required text and dragging it to the new position. Double clicking here also expands and collapses text.*

17. Collapse the heading again and click **Move Down**, 🔳, to move it back to its original position between **Background** and **Security**.

18. The **Promote** button, 🔳, is used to move the text up a style. The **Demote** button, 🔳, is used to move the text down a style.

19. Select the main title **E-Commerce**, which is **Level 1** and click **Demote**, 🔳, to change it to **Level 2**.

20. Collapse all of the remaining paragraphs. Select each of the subheadings in turn (**Level 2**) and **Demote** them to **Level 3**.

> ℹ️ *There is no style defined for level 3 or lower so internal default styles will be applied. It is advisable to define styles for all levels that will be used.*

21. Check what has happened in **Print Layout** view. Switch to **Outline View** and demote the subheadings to **Level 4**.

22. Now **Promote** the subheadings to **Level 1** using either the **Promote** button, 🔳, or the **Promote to Heading 1** button, 🔳.

23. Experiment. Try promoting and demoting different headings and then close the document <u>without</u> saving the changes.

Driving Lesson 18 - Multilevel Lists

▣ Park and Read

Styles for bulleted or numbered lists can be created to contain up to nine levels. A different format can be assigned to each level.

⌐ Manoeuvres

1. Start a new document. From the **Home** tab, select **Multilevel List** ▦

2. From the bottom of the list, select **Define a New Multilevel List**.

3. From here, individual levels can be modified.

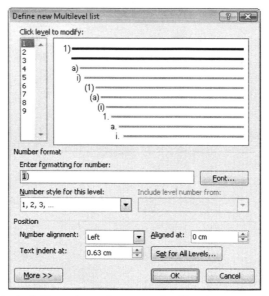

4. Level **1** is selected. Drop down the arrow for **Number style for this level**. Select Bullet: * . If this is not shown, click **New Bullet** and from the **Symbol** dialog box choose * and click **OK**.

5. Click on **2** from **Click level to modify**. Choose a **Number style** of Bullet: ⇒ . If not shown follow step 4 to select the symbol and click **OK**.

6. Click on **3** from **Click level to modify**. Choose a **Number style** click **New Bullet** and from the **Symbol** dialog box, choose **Symbol 197**
     and click **OK**.

☞

Driving Lesson 18 - Continued

7. Click 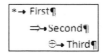 and in the **Font** dialog box, change the **Font color** to **Red** and click **OK**.

8. Click **OK** again and the first level bullet is applied

9. Type **First**, press **<Enter>**, **Second <Enter>**, **Third <Enter>**.

10. The levels are not apparent at the moment. Click in front of **Second** and press **<Tab>**.

11. Click in front of **Third** and press **<Tab>** twice.

```
*→ First¶
  ⇒→Second¶
    ⊕→ Third¶
```

12. Click on the page, away from the list or press **<Enter>** until the bullets are no longer applied. A multi-level number style is to be created.

13. Click on the **Multilevel List** button.

14. From the **List** Library, select an offset **Number Style** of **1, 1.1, 1.1.1...**.

15. The list is applied. To redefine the list, with the number still selected, drop the **Multilevel list** down again and select **Define a New Multilevel List**.

16. The chosen style is available for modification. Click on  and change the **Start at** number to **1**.

17. Leave **Level 1** as it is, but change the  **Eont...** for **Level 2** to **Lucida Handwriting** and **Level 3** to **Bradley Hand ITC** (choose alternative fonts if these are unavailable).

18. Click **OK** twice to return to the document.

19. Create a list as for the bullets.

20. Use **<Tab>** to create the three levels.

```
1→ First¶
  1.1  →    Second¶
    1.1.1→ Third¶
```

21. Close the document <u>without</u> saving.

Driving Lesson 19 - Revision: Paragraph Editing

This is not an ECDL test. Testing may only be carried out through certified ECDL test centres. This covers the features introduced in this section. Try not to refer to the preceding Driving Lessons while completing it.

1. Open the document **Stately Home**.

2. Change the **Style** of the main heading to **Heading1** and the subheadings to **Heading 3**.

3. Create a new style (**Body**) for the body text, based on **Normal**, with the font as **Tahoma 11pt** and justified with line spacing of **1.5 lines**.

4. Apply the **Body** style to all body text.

5. In **Outline View**, promote all the subheadings to **Heading 2**.

6. Apply a paragraph setting to paragraph 1 of **The Gardens**, so that it will always be kept with the next paragraph.

7. Apply a paragraph setting to the **Pets' Corner** heading so that a new page will be created before it.

8. Save the document as **Stately Home2** and close it.

If you experienced any difficulty completing this Revision refer back to the Driving Lessons in this section. Then redo the Revision.

Once you are confident with the features, complete the Record of Achievement Matrix referring to the section at the end of the guide. Only when competent move on to the next Section.

Section 4
Document Setup

By the end of this Section you should be able to:

Add and Delete Section Breaks

Apply Section Formatting

Apply Headers and Footers to Sections

Create Multiple Columns in a Document

Modify Column Layout, Width and Spacing

Create Watermarks

To gain an understanding of the above features, work through the **Driving Lessons** in this **Section**.

For each **Driving Lesson**, read the **Park and Read** instructions, without touching the keyboard, then work through the numbered steps of the **Manoeuvres** on the computer. Complete the **Revision Exercise(s)** at the end of the section to test your knowledge.

Driving Lesson 20 - Adding/Deleting Section Breaks

▣ Park and Read

When certain pages or parts of a document are to be formatted differently from the rest, e.g. page layout or page numbering, sections are created. Each section can have its own page layout and headers and footers (see later Driving Lesson). A document can have as many sections as required.

↱ Manoeuvres

1. Open the document **Stately Home**. Change to **Draft** view so you can see the breaks on screen.

2. Position the cursor in front of **The Gardens**.

3. From the **Page Layout** tab, select **Breaks** from the **Page Setup** group. From **Section Breaks**, choose **Continuous**, i.e. it will not start a new page.

ℹ️ *Even page and Odd page Section breaks will insert a break and start the next section on the next odd or even numbered page of a document.*

> **Section Breaks**
>
> **Next Page**
> Insert a section break and start the new section on the next page.
>
> **Continuous**
> Insert a section break and start the new section on the same page.

4. Insert a **Next Page** section break in front of **Pets' Corner**.

5. Section breaks can be changed. The first section break should have been a **Next Page** break. To change it, click in the **Gardens** paragraph and from the **Page Layout** tab, display the **Page Setup** dialog box.

6. Select the **Layout** tab and click the **Section start:** drop down arrow. Select **New page** and click **OK**. The break is changed and the **Gardens** section is now on a separate page.

7. Click in the **Gardens** paragraph, from the **Page Layout** tab, click the **Orientation** button and select **Landscape**.

8. Scroll through the document to see that only the pages of the **Gardens** section are in landscape.

9. Click in each section break in turn and press <**Delete**>. The breaks are removed and the document reverts to its original appearance.

10. Close the document <u>without</u> saving, so that recent changes are lost.

Driving Lesson 21 - Applying Section Formatting

▣ Park and Read

Once sections have been created in a document, each one can be formatted in a different way. For example, the page layout of one section could be in portrait and another in landscape. Other settings like margins, vertical alignment, headers and footers and columns can also be modified from section to section (columns and headers and footers are described in later exercises).

Manoeuvres

1. Open the document **Stately Home**.

2. Insert continuous section breaks before the following paragraphs: **The House**, **The Gardens, Pets' Corner** and **Gift Shop**.

3. With the cursor in the **Pets' Corner** paragraph, display the **Page Layout** tab, click **Margins** and select **Custom Margins**. Set the **Left** and **Right** margins to **5 cm**.

4. Make sure **Apply to** shows **This section** and click **OK**. The new margins are applied to this section only. This emphasises the section.

5. Click anywhere in the **House** section and display the **Layout** tab in the **Page Setup** dialog box. Click the **Section start:** drop down arrow and select **New page**.

6. Click **OK**. The break at the start of the **House** section is changed.

7. Click in the **Gardens** section and repeat the process to change the section break at the end of the **House** section to a **New page** break. The **House** section is now on a separate page.

8. Click anywhere in the **House** section, display the **Page Setup** dialog box, **Layout** tab. Click the **Vertical alignment** drop down and select **Center**.

9. Click **OK** and the section is positioned in the centre of the page.

10. Preview the document to show the changes to page **2** and page **4**.

11. Close the document <u>without</u> saving.

Driving Lesson 22 - Section Headers and Footers

🅿 Park and Read

Each section in a document can have different headers and footers. This guide has a different header for each section. Headers and footers can be omitted from the first page of a document if desired and different ones can be applied to odd and even pages.

☞ Manoeuvres

1.   Open the document **Headers**. This file consists of a front page and four chapters, to which individual headers and footers are to be applied (ignore the repeated text - this is for demonstration only).

2.   Insert continuous section breaks on: page **1** after **...stately home**, page **3** end of final paragraph, page **7** end of the last paragraph, page **11** end of last paragraph.

3.   Go to page **1** and select the **Page Setup** launcher from the **Page Layout** tab.

4.   In the **Headers and footers** section, check **Different odd and even** and **Different first page**. There is to be no number on page **1**.

```
Headers and footers
    ☑ Different odd and even
    ☑ Different first page
```

5.   Make sure **Apply to** under **Preview** displays **Whole document**, if not use the drop down arrow to select it. Click **OK**.

6.   From the **Insert** tab, select **Footer** and **Edit Footer**. On page **1** there is only to be a footer with a centred date.

7.   Press **<Tab>** to move to the centre.

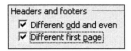

8.   Click **Date and Time**, 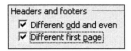, and choose a suitable format to insert the current date. Click on **Go to Header**.

9.   Click **Next Section**, [🔲 Next Section], to move to the even page header for section 2 and click **Link to Previous**, [🔲 Link to Previous], to break the automatic link to the first page header.

Driving Lesson 22 - Continued

10. With the cursor at the left of the header, change the font to **Arial** and type **History**. Make the text bold.

11. Go to the footer and at the left click **Page Number**, [Page Number ▾]. Select **Current Position** and then **Plain Number** from the options.

12. Click [Link to Previous] again to remove the link.

13. Go to the header and move to the header for the odd pages. Break the automatic link.

14. Press **<Tab>** twice to move to the right and type **History**. Format again as **Arial** and make it **bold**.

15. Switch to the footer and at the right of this footer, insert page numbers, making sure the link to the previous section is broken.

16. Continue to create different headers for each section, breaking the link to previous sections as appropriate (there is no need to break the link in the footer once the page numbers are established).

17. For **Chapter 2** headers, the text **The House** should be at the right on odd pages and at the left on even pages. For the other chapter headings use **Pets Corner** and **Gardens**.

18. When you have completed all the headers and footers, close the **Header and Footer** view and scroll through the document, checking that page **1** is different from the rest and that all odd and even pages are correct for each chapter.

19. Save the document as **Headers2** and close it.

Driving Lesson 23 - Multiple Column Layout

▣ Park and Read

Columns divide the page vertically. Several columns can be created on a page to create a varied effect. Columns can be applied to the whole document, or to certain parts of it.

☞ Manoeuvres

1. Start a new document and type the text **Daily News**. This will become a **Masthead** (a title that spans the page).

2. Centre the text and change the font to **Rockwell Extra Bold** (or another bold font if this is not available). Make the text large enough to fill a large part of the top line but not so large that it moves on to two lines, e.g. **60pt**.

3. Press **<Enter>** after the **Masthead**, change the font size to **12pt** and click the **Align Left** button, ⬛.

4. From the **Page Layout** tab insert a **Continuous** section break to separate it from the text that is to be inserted.

5. Select the **Insert** tab and from the **Text** group click the arrow on the **Object** button, 🔲 Object ▾. Select **Text from File** and insert the data file **Articles**.

6. With the cursor at the beginning of this text, display the **Page Layout** tab and click the **Columns** button, ⬛ Columns ▾. Select **More columns**.

7. Select **Two** from the **Presets** area and make sure the **Apply to** area shows **This section**.

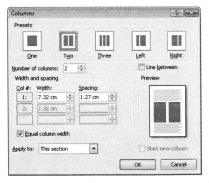

8. Check the **Line between** box to divide the columns with a line and click **OK** to apply the columns (if you are in **Draft View**, *Word* automatically changes to **Print Layout View**).

9. Save the document as **Columns** and leave it open.

Driving Lesson 24 - Modifying Column Layout

▣ Park and Read

Columns can be balanced to divide the text evenly. **Column breaks** are used so that the following text is moved to the top of the next column.

↱ Manoeuvres

1. Use the document **Columns**. Make sure **Show/Hide** ⟦¶⟧, is <u>on</u>.

2. To place the article about the dog at the top of the second column, place the insertion point before the **D** of **Dog**.

3. Click ⟦ Breaks ⟧ from the **Page Layout** tab and click on **Column**. The column break appears as a dotted line across the screen.

> The·man's·account·was·so·horrifying,·that·
> police·are·warning·members·of·the·public·
> to·stay·away·from·the·local·woods·until·
> further·investigations·have·been·made.¶
>
> ······················· Column Break ·······················

4. Click ⟦ Columns ▾ ⟧ and select **Three** from the list to change the number of columns to **3**. Use a column break to move the **Fundraiser** story to the top of the third column.

5. Print the document.

6. Click on the first column break and press **<Delete>** to remove it then delete the remaining column break and switch to **Print Layout** view to see the changes.

7. Close the document <u>without</u> saving to lose the recent changes.

8. Re-open the **Columns** document.

9. To balance the text in the columns, position the cursor at the end of the text, after the word **proceeds** and insert a **Continuous** section break.

10. Preview the document. The text should now be equally divided between the two columns.

11. With the cursor in the text, change the number of columns to **3**.

12. Preview the document. The text is still evenly distributed because of the section break.

13. Save the document as **Columns2** and leave it open.

Driving Lesson 25 - Modifying Column Width/Spacing

▣ Park and Read

After columns have been applied to a document, it is possible to change the column width and the spacing between columns.

⌐ Manoeuvres

1. Using the document **Columns2**, click at the beginning of the first column of text.

2. Display the **Columns** dialog box and remove the check from the **Equal column width** box in **Width and spacing**.

3. To change the column widths, amend the measurements in the **Width** boxes to match the following diagram.

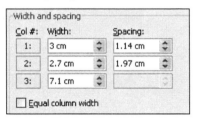

ℹ️ *The **Spacing** will vary depending on the settings of the printer attached to your PC.*

4. Notice how the **Preview** changes to show the new column widths.

5. Click **OK** to apply the changes.

6. To change the spacing between the three columns, display the **Columns** dialog box again.

7. Change the **Spacing** measurements to match the following diagram.

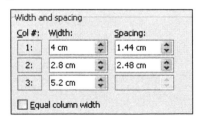

8. Click **OK**.

9. Notice the effect on the document, then close it without saving the changes.

Driving Lesson 26 - Creating a Watermark

P Park and Read

A watermark is a piece of text or an image appearing in the background of a document, usually on every page. These can be easily created in *Word*. Watermarks are meant for printed documents only. Watermark text is stored in the Header or Footer of a document.

Manoeuvres

1. Open the document **Wine**.

2. Select the **Page Layout** tab and click **Watermark**. Click **Custom Watermark**, then **Text Watermark** and change the **Text** to **SAMPLE** using the drop down list (text can also be typed into the box).

i *Selecting the **Watermark** button also shows a list of preset text watermarks. Clicking on one of them would apply it.*

3. Leave all other settings the same.

Department Section	Stock Ref.	Description	Price £'s
White Wine	A11	Entre deux Mers	3.50
	A12	Trebbiano	3.99
	A13	Frascati	2.99
	A14	Mâcon Villages	3.99
Red Wine	B11	Chateauneuf du Pape	8.99
	B12	Beaujolais	3.99
	B13	Chianti	4.25
	B14	Rioja	5.00
Rose Wine	C11	Mateus Rose	3.75
	C12	Rose D'Anjou	3.99
	C13	Zinfandel	4.50
	C14	Corbon	2.75
Wine Boxes	D11	Reisling	7.99
	D12	Soave	9.99
	D13	Burgundy	12.99
	D14	Côtes du Rhone	11.20
Beers	E11	McEwans Export	0.49
	E12	Lorimers Scotch	0.45
	E13	Newcastle Brown	0.65
	E14	Whitbread Trophy	0.50
Lagers	F11	Red Stripe	0.89
	F12	Fosters	0.70
	F13	Carlsberg	0.75
	F14	Castlemaine XXXX	0.80

4. Click **OK**.

5. The **Watermark** is added to the header as **WordArt**. Display the **Header** and click on the text **SAMPLE** in the centre of the screen.

6. Close the **Header**.

7. Print the document.

8. Leave the document open for the next Driving Lesson.

Driving Lesson 27 - Modifying and Deleting Watermarks

P Park and Read

After adding a watermark it can be modified by changing the text or by selecting to add a **Picture Watermark** using the **Select Picture** button. **Watermarks** are removed by selecting the **No watermark** option in the **Printed Watermark** dialog box.

Manoeuvres

1. The document **Wine** should still be open. If not, open it.

2. From the **Page Layout** tab, click **Watermark**, then click **Custom Watermark**. The **Printed Watermark** dialog box is displayed.

3. A text watermark is modified by changing the contents of the **Text** box either by entering new text, amending the text already there or by selecting different text from the drop down list. Select the **Text watermark** option, click the drop down list and select **CONFIDENTIAL**. Click **OK**, the watermark has been modified.

4. To insert a picture, display the **Printed Watermark** dialog box.

5. Select the **Picture watermark** option and then click **Select Picture** and locate the data files from **Look in**. Select the **watermark** file and click **Insert**.

6. In the **Printed Watermark** dialog box, ensure **Washout** is checked so the graphic is not too vivid.

7. Click **OK**. Print a copy of the document.

8. To delete a watermark display the **Printed Watermark** dialog box. Select the **No watermark** option and click **OK**. All types of watermark can be removed in this way.

9. Close the document <u>without</u> saving.

Driving Lesson 28 - Revision: Document Setup

This is not an ECDL test. Testing may only be carried out through certified ECDL test centres. This covers the features introduced in this section. Try not to refer to the preceding Driving Lessons while completing it.

1.　　Open the document **Predators**.

2.　　Insert **Continuous** section breaks in front of the **Body Form** title and before the **Conclusion**.

3.　　Insert a **Next Page** section break before the **Senses** section.

4.　　Change the left and right margins to **4 cm** in the **Senses** section only.

5.　　Apply 2 columns from **Body Form** to **Methods of Reproduction**.

6.　　Reduce the spacing between the columns to **1cm**.

7.　　Apply headers and footers of your choice, but make sure that the first page header and those for odd and even pages are different.

8.　　Apply a diagonal text watermark, **DO NOT COPY**, to the document.

9.　　Print the document.

10.　Close it <u>without</u> saving.

If you experienced any difficulty completing this Revision refer back to the Driving Lessons in this section. Then redo the Revision.

Once you are confident with the features, complete the Record of Achievement Matrix referring to the section at the end of the guide. Only when competent move on to the next Section.

Section 5
Tables

By the end of this Section you should be able to:

AutoFormat Tables

Merge and Split Cells

Convert Text to a Table

Sort Data

Perform Calculations

Change Table Properties and Setup

To gain an understanding of the above features, work through the **Driving Lessons** in this **Section**.

For each **Driving Lesson**, read the **Park and Read** instructions, without touching the keyboard, then work through the numbered steps of the **Manoeuvres** on the computer. Complete the **Revision Exercise(s)** at the end of the section to test your knowledge.

Driving Lesson 29 - Table Styles

▣ Park and Read

You can quickly give your table a professional design by using one of *Word*'s built-in table formats. You can also create your own table style.

⌕ Manoeuvres

1. Open the document **Staffing**.

2. Place the cursor within the table and select the **Design** tab from **Table Tools**. Move the cursor over the styles in the **Table Styles** group to see the effect.

3. Click on the **More** arrow in **Table Styles**.

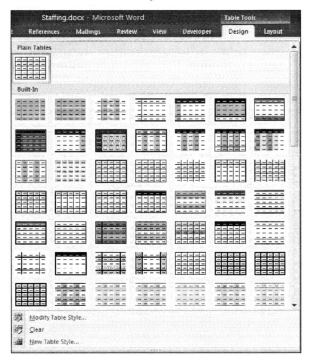

4. Click on any style to apply it to the table. Try different examples.

ℹ️ *To create a new table style, click the **New Table Style** button in the **Table Styles** drop down and choose the required settings. The new style will then appear in the **Custom** area of the **Table Styles** list.*

5. Save the document as **Staffing2** and close it.

Driving Lesson 30 - Merging & Splitting Cells

▣ Park and Read

Cells in a table can be **merged** or **split**. To merge cells means to join two or more cells together to make one large cell. To split cells means to divide a cell into two or more cells.

⌐ Manoeuvres

1. In a new document, create a table with **5** columns and **10** rows.

2. Move the cursor to the second cell on the top line, select that cell and the cell to the right of it. Select the **Layout** tab (under **Table Tools**). Click **Merge Cells**. ⊞ Merge Cells . The cells are merged.

3. Merge the two cells at the right of the top row then all of the cells on the second row.

4. Merge cells 1 and 2 on rows 3 to 9. This must be done one row at a time.

5. Merge cells 1 to 4 on the bottom row.

6. Your employer wants you to keep a record of daily sales to keep in your Personal Development folder. Enter text into the table until it matches the diagram below.

Date	Name		Department	
Product		Price	Quantity	Total Price
Grand Total				

7. Your employer has decided to add product reference numbers to the table. Position the cursor in the cell containing **Product** and click **Split Cells** ⊞ Split Cells , from the **Merge** group in **Layout**.

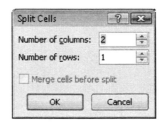

Driving Lesson 30 - Continued

8.   Make sure **2 columns** and **1 row** are selected from the **Split Cells** dialog box and click **OK**.

9.   Enter **Ref.** in the cell to the right of **Product** and split the cells in the six rows below.

Date	Name		Department	
Product	Ref.	Price	Quantity	Total Price
Grand Total				

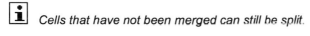

Cells that have not been merged can still be split.

10.   Save the document as **Sales Checklist** and close it.

Driving Lesson 31 - Converting Text to a Table

▣ Park and Read

Existing text can be converted to table format, providing the text is already separated into fields. This can be done with commas, tabs or paragraph marks. It may be necessary to remove any extra commas or tabs to reach the required format.

↱ Manoeuvres

1. Open the document **Diary**. Select all of the text.

2. Select the **Insert** tab and click **Table**.

3. Click Convert Text to Table.

4. The **Number of columns** is calculated from the number of fields in the first line of the text, this should be correct. Check that **Separate text at** selection shows **Tabs** and click **OK**.

5. The text will now be in table format. Apply any **Table Style** to the table, as desired.

6. Save the document as **Converted** and close it.

ℹ️ *To convert a table into text, select the table and display the **Layout** tab. Click* **Convert to Text,** ⊞ Convert to Text *. From the **Convert Table to Text** dialog box, choose how the text is to be separated. Click **OK**.*

Driving Lesson 32 - Sorting Table Data

▣ Park and Read

A table can be sorted in order of any column, with secondary sorts being applied, if required. Ascending or descending sorts can be performed on text or numbers.

☞ Manoeuvres

1. Open the document **Vacation**. This shows the holiday entitlement of staff members.

2. Make sure the cursor is within the table. Select the **Layout** tab from **Table Tools**.

3. From the **Data** group, click **Sort** to display the **Sort** dialog box.

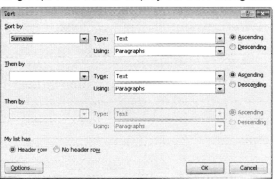

4. Check that **Header row** is selected in the **My list has** area. The **Sort by** choices will now show the column headings.

5. Select **Surname** and **Ascending**. Click **OK** to sort the table by surname, **A-Z**.

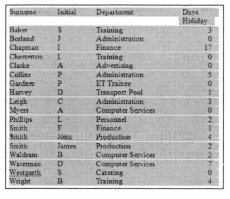

Surname	Initial	Department	Days Holiday
Baker	S	Training	3
Borland	J	Administration	0
Chapman	I	Finance	17
Chesterton	I	Training	0
Clarke	A	Advertising	0
Collins	P	Administration	5
Gardner	P	ET Trainee	0
Harvey	D	Transport Pool	1
Leigh	C	Administration	3
Myers	A	Computer Services	0
Phillips	L	Personnel	2
Smith	F	Finance	1
Smith	John	Production	4
Smith	James	Production	2
Waldram	B	Computer Services	2
Waterman	D	Computer Services	7
Westgarth	S	Catering	0
Wright	B	Training	4

Driving Lesson 32 - Continued

6. Now, with the cursor in the table, click **Sort** again. Select **Surname** and **Descending**, then click **OK** to sort by surnames **Z-A**.

Surname	Initial	Department	Days Holiday
Wright	B	Training	4
Westgarth	S	Catering	0
Waterman	D	Computer Services	7
Waldram	B	Computer Services	2
Smith	F	Finance	1
Smith	John	Production	4
Smith	James	Production	2
Phillips	L	Personnel	2
Myers	A	Computer Services	0
Leigh	C	Administration	3
Harvey	D	Transport Pool	1
Gardner	P	ET Trainee	0
Collins	P	Administration	5
Clarke	A	Advertising	0
Chesterton	I	Training	0
Chapman	I	Finance	17
Borland	J	Administration	0
Baker	S	Training	3

7. Again, with the cursor within the table, click **Sort**. From the **Sort by** selection, choose **Days Holiday**, **Descending** and click **OK** (note that the **Type** changes to **Number**).

Surname	Initial	Department	Days Holiday
Chapman	I	Finance	17
Waterman	D	Computer Services	7
Collins	P	Administration	5
Wright	B	Training	4
Smith	John	Production	4
Leigh	C	Administration	3
Baker	S	Training	3
Waldram	B	Computer Services	2
Smith	James	Production	2
Phillips	L	Personnel	2
Smith	F	Finance	1
Harvey	D	Transport Pool	1
Westgarth	S	Catering	0
Myers	A	Computer Services	0
Gardner	P	ET Trainee	0
Clarke	A	Advertising	0
Chesterton	I	Training	0
Borland	J	Administration	0

8. Repeat this sort, adding **Surname**, **Ascending** in the **Then by** section. Select **OK** to sort the list by the amount of holidays, then **A-Z** by surname.

9. Who is last on the list?

10. Save the document as **Vacation2**, obtain a printed copy and close it.

☒ *Blank rows in a table will be sorted along with the data. It may be prudent to remove them and then replace, if necessary, after sorting.*

☒ *See the **Answers** section at the end of the guide.*

Driving Lesson 33 - Performing Calculations

▣ Park and Read

Calculations can be carried out within a table. A column of numbers can be summed, or any basic calculation can be performed on the data within the table. Every formula must start with the equals sign **=**. Standard mathematical functions are used to create formulas.

Like a spreadsheet, each column in a table is referred to by a letter: **A,B,C,D**, etc., whilst rows are referred to by numbers: **1**, **2**, **3**, **4**, etc. The cell address, e.g. **A1**, is the position where the row and column intersect. It is this cell address that will be used to build formulas, e.g. **=A1 + A2**.

↱ Manoeuvres

1. Create a **5 x 5** table in a new document, and in the first column (column **A**) enter a list of four numbers.

2. With the cursor in the last cell of the column, display the **Layout** tab from **Table Tools** and click **ƒ× Formula**. The formula dialog box suggests an appropriate formula.

   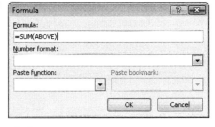

3. In this case **SUM** field code is required. Use the **Number format** drop down to select **0.00**, click **OK** and the sum is complete with 2 decimal places.

4. With the field code highlighted, click **ƒ× Formula** and using the **Number format** drop down, select **0**, a format with no decimal places. Click **OK** to apply the different number format.

5. Place the cursor in cell **B2**. Click **Formula**. Delete the suggested formula and enter **=a1*a2**. Click **OK** and the answer will be displayed.

6. In cell **B3** use the same method to calculate **a2/a1**.

7. To calculate the **Product** of the above two cells, with the cursor in **B4**, open the **Formula** dialog box and remove the suggested formula. Type **=**.

8. From the drop down list under **Paste function**, select **Product**.

9. In the brackets insert **B2,B3**. The formula should read **=PRODUCT(B2,B3)**, the equivalent of **B2*B3**. Click **OK** to perform the calculation.

10. Close the document <u>without</u> saving.

🛈 *If any numbers are changed, formulas are not automatically updated. To recalculate any formula, select it and press <F9>.*

Driving Lesson 34 - Table Properties and Setup

▣ Park and Read

Various aspects of a table can be changed, for example the cell margins, text alignment and direction. If the table is large, you can apply settings so that the heading rows are repeated on each page, or so that rows either break or don't break across pages.

↱ Manoeuvres

1. Open the document **Company** and select the top row of the table - the text direction is to be changed.

2. Select the **Layout** tab from **Table Tools**. From the **Alignment** group,

    select **Text Direction** .

3. The text can now be read downwards. Click **Text Direction** again.

4. The downward direction is changed. Click **Text Direction** again.

5. The text is returned to its original position.

6. The top row of the table is now too large and the other rows could be wider. Click on the table select icon, ⊞, at the top left corner to select the whole table.

7. Click on the **Layout** tab. Click the **Properties** button in the **Table** group. In the **Table Properties** dialog box, select the **Row** tab.

8. From **Size**, check **Specify height** and enter **1 cm** in the box. Ensure **At least** is selected.

    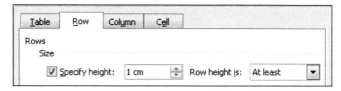

9. Click **OK**.

10. With the whole table still selected, display the **Table Properties** dialog box again. The column width can also be altered from here. Click on the **Row** and then the **Column** tabs to review the information.

Driving Lesson 34 - Continued

11. Select the **Cell** tab. Click **Options**.

12. In **Cell Options** remove the check from **Same as the whole table** so that the margins can be set manually. Change the **Top** cell margin to **0.2cm** (to move the text down in every cell).

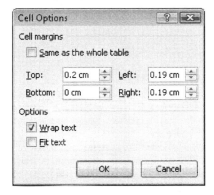

13. Click **OK**, then **OK** again to see the effect.

14. With the whole table still selected, display the **Table Properties** dialog box again. From the **Cell** tab, in the **Vertical alignment** section, the available options are **Top**, **Center** and **Bottom**. Select **Bottom** alignment and click **OK**. The text is moved to the bottom of each cell.

15. Place the cursor in front of the surname on the bottom row on page **1**. Press <**Enter**> until the text moves to the next page. This row has been split across 2 pages.

16. Select the table and display **Table Properties**. On the **Row** tab, notice **Allow row to break across pages** is checked.

17. Clear the check and click **OK**. Notice that all the data from the row is now back together.

18. Remove the paragraph marks added previously, the row moves back to page 1.

19. If a table is split over more than one page it's a good idea to have headings on each page. Select the top row and make it **bold**.

20. With the top row still selected, display the **Table Properties** and the **Row** tab.

21. Check **Repeat as header row at the top of each page**. Click **OK**.

22. Check the top of each page to see the header row.

23. Save the document as **Company2** and close it.

Driving Lesson 35 - Revision: Tables

This is not an ECDL test. Testing may only be carried out through certified ECDL test centres. This covers the features introduced in this section. Try not to refer to the preceding Driving Lessons while completing it.

1. Start a new document.

2. Create a new table to match the table below, an invoice (you will need to merge cells).

Invoice				
Ref No	Description	Qty	Price	Total
Subtotal				
VAT				
Total				

3. Print the document and close it <u>without</u> saving.

4. Open the document **Quotas**.

5. Convert the text to a table (separated at tabs).

6. Calculate the total sales for each salesperson.

7. Print the document and close it <u>without</u> saving.

8. Start a new document and create a **4x6** table containing a list of five types of car.

9. The headings should be **Manufacturer**, **Model**, **Colour** and **Price**.

10. Enter a fictional price for each car.

11. Sort the table in ascending alphabetical order by model.

12. Now sort the table numerically by price, from highest to lowest.

13. Sort the table alphabetically by **Colour**.

14. Save the document as **Car sort** and close it.

If you experienced any difficulty completing this Revision refer back to the Driving Lessons in this section. Then redo the Revision.

Once you are confident with the features, complete the Record of Achievement Matrix referring to the section at the end of the guide. Only when competent move on to the next Section.

Section 6
Referencing

By the end of this Section you should be able to:

Create, Modify & Delete Footnotes & Endnotes

Create, Format & Update a Table of Contents

Add & Delete Bookmarks

Create & Delete Cross-references

Add Captions

Create a Table of Figures

Create & Edit Index Entries

To gain an understanding of the above features, work through the **Driving Lessons** in this **Section**.

For each **Driving Lesson**, read the **Park and Read** instructions, without touching the keyboard, then work through the numbered steps of the **Manoeuvres** on the computer. Complete the **Revision Exercise(s)** at the end of the section to test your knowledge.

Driving Lesson 36 - Creating Footnotes and Endnotes

▣ Park and Read

Footnotes are a formalised way of documenting sources for quotations, facts and ideas in a report. A footnote number is automatically placed in the document next to the text to be referenced. The same number appears at the bottom of the page with details about the source of the information. **Endnotes** perform the same function, but are found at the end of a document.

↱ Manoeuvres

1. Open the document **Discovery**.

2. To create a footnote, position the cursor after **tomb** in the second paragraph and select the **References** tab, then click **Insert Footnote**.

3. The cursor moves to the bottom of the page, ready for the text to be entered into a special footnote area. Enter the following text: **Evidence was found of early grave robbers**.

4. Use the scroll bar to move back to the main document and notice how the **reference mark**, the number **1**, has been inserted in the correct place.

5. Insert the following footnotes:

    Paragraph **2**, after **Howard Carter**: **Lord Caernarvon financed the dig.**.

    Paragraph **3**, after **canopic jars**: **Alabaster or clay pots with the heads of Egyptian deities for lids. Each watched over a particular body part.**.

    Paragraph **4**, after **bandaged body**: **Jewels and other precious items were found in the wrappings.**.

6. Move the mouse over the reference mark **1** to display the footnote as a caption.

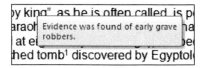

7. Save the document as **Noted** and close it.

8. Open **Discovery** again.

Driving Lesson 36 - Continued

9.   Insert a page break before the fourth paragraph.

10.   Position the cursor after **tomb** in the second paragraph and select **References** and then click .

11.   Enter the same text as in step **3**. Note that it is entered at the end of the whole document.

12.   Insert the notes described in step **5** as **Endnotes**.

[i] *Endnotes* *have their own number sequence, separate from* *Footnotes*. *It would be confusing to have both in the same document.*

13.   Print the document.

14.   Endnotes can be converted to footnotes and vice versa. Click the dialog box launcher in the **Footnotes** group. At the **Footnote and Endnote** dialog box, click **Convert**.

Convert Notes
● Convert all footnotes to endnotes
○ Convert all endnotes to footnotes
○ Swap footnotes and endnotes
OK   Cancel

15.   Ensure **Convert all endnotes to footnotes** is selected and click **OK**.

16.   Click **Close**. Footnotes have replaced the endnotes.

17.   To convert them back to endnotes, open the **Footnote and Endnote** dialog box and click **Convert**.

18.   Select **Convert all footnotes to endnotes** and click **OK**, then click **Close**.

19.   Save it as **Endnotes** and close it.

Driving Lesson 37 - Modifying/Deleting Footnotes and Endnotes

P Park and Read

Footnotes and endnotes can be edited, formatted and deleted in the same way as normal text. There is a widely observed convention that footnote reference numbers are entered in superscript form.

Manoeuvres

1. Open the file **Birds**. This document contains four footnotes.

2. From the **References** tab, click **Show Notes** from the **Footnotes** group. The footnotes are displayed at the bottom of the page.

3. Click **Show Notes** again and the **Footnote 1** reference in the text is displayed. Move the cursor over the **Footnote 1** reference and read the caption.

4. Move the cursor over the **Footnote 2** reference, read the caption then double click. The insertion point is moved to the start of the second footnote at the bottom of the page.

5. There is a mistake in the second footnote, the food referred to is **fat balls** and not **fatballs**. Edit the text as required.

i *Double click on a reference number in the text to go directly to a footnote or endnote.*

6. Select the first reference mark in the text and then delete it. The footnote text is also removed and the remaining footnotes are automatically renumbered.

i *If a footnote is deleted, the footnote reference mark is not removed. However, if the reference mark is deleted, the corresponding footnote is removed along with it. Great care, therefore, must be exercised when removing footnote reference marks.*

7. Use **Print Preview** to check the appearance of the document.

8. Print a copy of the document and close it <u>without</u> saving the changes.

Driving Lesson 38 - Creating a Table of Contents

▣ Park and Read

It is possible in *Word* to create various reference features in a document such as **tables of contents**, **indexes**, **cross references**, and **captions**. Once these tables are created, they can automatically be updated, if any of the information is changed.

A table of contents is based on styles within a document. Certain heading styles are chosen, and all text in the document that uses these styles is automatically included in the contents.

↱ Manoeuvres

1. Open **Topperville Hall**. This document has already been formatted with **Heading** styles.

2. Place the cursor on the blank line below the title, press **<Enter>**, type **Contents** and press **<Enter>** again.

3. Place the cursor on the blank line below **Contents** and select the **References** tab and click **Table of Contents**. Select **Insert Table of Contents**.

ℹ *If the **Table of Contents** is being created from newly created styles, click the **Options** button to specify the order of styles being used. From **Available styles**, remove the level numbers and insert the correct number next to the required style. To check that the table shows the correct styles at the correct level, look at the **Preview** before clicking **OK**.*

4. To see different formats applied to the **Table of Contents**, choose each type in turn from the **Formats** drop down list. The preview shows the effects.

5. Select **Formal**, then click **OK** to create a table of contents.

History of Topperville Hall

Contents

INTRODUCTION 1

THE HOUSE 1
   GUIDED TOUR 1
    Museum of Childhood 1

THE GARDENS 2
   Hidden Secrets 2
   The Fountain 3
   The Maze 3

PETS' CORNER 3

GIFT SHOP 3

TEA ROOM 4

OPENING TIMES 4

6. Save the document as **Contents** and leave it open.

Driving Lesson 39 - Updating a Table of Contents

▣ Park and Read

Once a table of contents has been created, it is an easy matter to update it if any changes are made to the contents themselves.

⌐ Manoeuvres

1. The **Contents** document should still be open. If not, open it.

2. To check that the page numbers are correct, hold down **<Ctrl>** and click on a page number in the table of contents. The cursor moves to the relevant place in the document.

3. Insert a **Page Break** before **Introduction** (**<Ctrl Enter>**). The page numbers in the contents are now incorrect.

4. To update the table of contents, click ⬚ Update Table .

5. When the **Update Table of Contents** dialog box appears, select the **Update page numbers only** option. Click **OK**.

6. Check the page numbers - they should now be correct.

ⓘ *Tables can be automatically updated prior to printing by setting the **Update fields before printing** option from **Word Options** then choosing **Display** and **Printing Options**.*

7. Save the document as **Contents** then close it.

Driving Lesson 40 - Adding and Deleting Bookmarks

🄿 Park and Read

A **bookmark** can be assigned to a text position or to a graphic within a document. Once a place within a document has been given a bookmark, there are various methods to locate it quickly and easily. This can be a very useful feature in a large, complex document.

☝ Manoeuvres

1. Open the file **Predators** and position the cursor on page **2**, at the beginning of the **Senses** heading.

2. Select the **Insert** tab and click **Bookmark**.

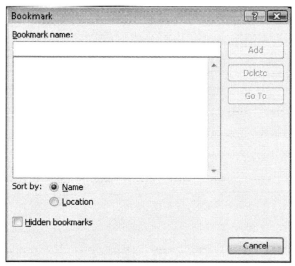

3. Enter **Senses** as the **Bookmark name**.

ℹ️ *A bookmark name cannot contain spaces.*

4. Click **Add** to create the bookmark.

5. Create a second, appropriately named bookmark for the **Conclusion** on page **3**.

6. Insert a suitable graphic of your choice from **Clip Art** after the **Diet** paragraph.

Driving Lesson 40 - Continued

7. Select the graphic, then click **Insert** and then click **Bookmark**.

8. Enter **sharkpic** as the **Bookmark name** and then click **Add**.

9. Select the first sentence of the **Teeth** paragraph and insert a bookmark named **toothache**.

10. Move the cursor to the beginning of the document.

11. Press **<F5>** to display the **Find and Replace** dialog box with the **Go To** tab selected.

> **i**   *Find and Replace can also be found on the **Home** tab.*

12. Select **Bookmark** from the **Go to what** box and the **Senses** bookmark from the bookmark name list.

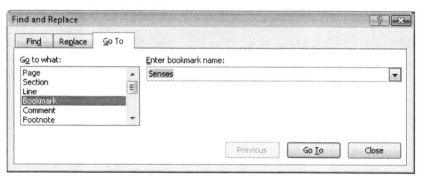

13. Click the **Go To** button to go to the **Senses** section. You may need to move the dialog box to see the result.

14. In the same way, move to the other bookmarked text and the graphic.

15. Close the **Find and Replace** dialog box.

16. To delete the **Senses** bookmark, in the **Links** group on the **Insert** tab, click **Bookmark**.

17. Select the **Senses** bookmark from the list.

18. Click the **Delete** button, then click **Close**.

19. Close the document <u>without</u> saving.

Driving Lesson 41 - Cross-Referencing

⊞ Park and Read

Cross-referencing is a method of placing a reference in a document, which refers to an item elsewhere in a document, such as a **heading**, **bookmark**, **caption**, etc. When a cross-reference is created there are a variety of options for the reference text, including page number, heading text, bookmark text, etc. If the cross reference is defined as a hyperlink, pressing <**Ctrl**> and clicking on it will take you directly to the target location.

Manoeuvres

1.   Open **References**. Various types of reference are to be created.

2.   Position the cursor after **Elizabeth I** in paragraph 1. Type (**Page** .

3.   On the **References** tab, select **Cross-reference**  from the **Captions** group. From **Reference type** choose **Bookmark**. A list of all the bookmarks can now be seen.

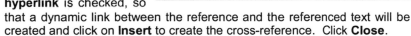

4.   From **Insert reference to** select **Page number** and **For which bookmark** highlight **Elizabeth**.

5.   Make sure **Insert as hyperlink** is checked, so that a dynamic link between the reference and the referenced text will be created and click on **Insert** to create the cross-reference. Click **Close**.

6.   Next to (**Page** the number **2** appears. Enter) after the number 2.

7.   Position the mouse pointer over the cross-reference page number, which has just been inserted - a caption appears, because the cross-reference was inserted as a hyperlink.

> Elizabeth
> **CTRL + click to follow link**

8.   Hold down <**Ctrl**> and click once to move to the associated paragraph.

Driving Lesson 41 - Continued

9. On page 1, place the cursor in the list after **The House**. Again type **(Page** and display the **Cross-reference** dialog box.

10. This time select **Heading** as the **Reference type** and insert the reference to **Page number**. Select the heading **The House**, click **Insert** and **Close**.

11. Complete the reference with a closing bracket **)**.

12. Create references like this for the remaining items in the list.

13. On page 1, place the cursor at the end of paragraph 1 and type **See further information in paragraph number** .

14. Insert a cross reference to a **Numbered item** and select item **1**.

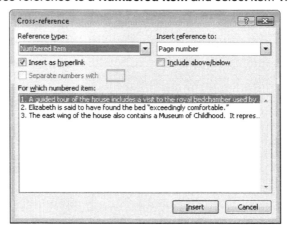

15. In **Insert reference to** select **Paragraph number**. Click **Insert** and close the **Cross-reference** dialog box. Complete the sentence with a full stop.

16. After the list, type **See opening times, page** and insert a cross reference to a **Table**, reference to **Page number** and choose the caption **Table 1**.

17. Move to page 2. Place the cursor after **from the tower** in the last paragraph, add a space and insert a cross reference.

18. Choose **Figure** as the **Reference type**, insert the reference to **Entire caption** and choose the caption **Figure 2**.

19. Try out the cross references.

20. Save the document as **Crossref** and leave it open.

 *To delete a cross-reference the field codes must be viewed. Select the **Office Button** and **Word Options**. From **Advanced**, locate the **Show document content** section. Check the **Show field codes instead of their values** box and click **OK**. Position the cursor in front of the cross reference to be deleted and press <**Delete**> twice. Remember to turn the field codes off afterwards.*

Driving Lesson 42 - Adding Numbered Captions

▣ Park and Read

Captions can be added individually to objects such as graphs, images and tables. They can also be set up to be automatically applied, so that when a graph, etc., is inserted, it is automatically numbered. Once captions have been entered in this way a **table of figures/captions** can also be created.

⬆ Manoeuvres

1. With **Crossref** still open from the previous lesson, move to the end of the document and press **<Enter>** to create a blank line.

2. Insert a **3 x 3** table and select it.

3. Select the **References** tab and then click **Insert Caption**. From **Label** choose **Table**. The caption can be positioned above or below the item. Select **Above selected item** in the **Position** box.

4. Click **OK**. The caption **Table 2** appears above the table, because Table 1 already exists.

5. Scroll up the document and position the cursor above the **Pets' Corner** paragraph and insert another 3 x 3 table.

6. Keeping the cursor within the table, insert a **Caption** and ensure the **Label** shows **Table**.

7. To change the caption text, enter **Events timetable** after the existing text. Click **OK**. The caption **Table 1 Events timetable** appears.

8. Scroll down to the other tables and notice they have been renumbered.

9. The pictures in the document all have captions except the one in the **Pets Corner** paragraph. Click on this picture and click **Insert Caption**.

10. Click the **Label** drop down, the default available options are; **Equation**, **Figure** and **Table**, but it is possible to add a new label to the list.

Driving Lesson 42 - Continued

11. Click the **New Label** button, enter **Image** and click **OK**.

12. Click **OK** to add **Image 1** as the caption label to this picture.

13. Select the caption and press <**Delete**> to remove it.

14. To delete the caption label, select the picture again. Display the **Caption** dialog box and click the **Delete Label** button. The label is deleted and the caption reverts back to **Figure**.

15. Click **OK**. The figure becomes **Figure 3** and all subsequent figures are renumbered accordingly.

16. To change the caption format, select any figure caption, click **Insert Caption**, and click the **Numbering** button.

17. In the **Caption Numbering** dialog box, drop down the **Format** options and select **A,B,C, ...**

18. Click **OK**, then click **Close** to close the **Caption** dialog box. All figure captions are changed.

19. **AutoCaptions** make it possible to automatically insert a caption relating to an object as soon as it is inserted into a document. Select **References** and click the **Insert Caption** button and then click **AutoCaption**. This shows a list of which inserted objects can have automatic captions assigned.

20. Scroll down the list and make sure that **Microsoft Word Table** is checked.

21. Click **OK** and insert a table anywhere in the document. Notice that a caption has automatically been created for it.

22. Apart from the table showing opening times, delete the other tables and captions. Ensure that the document still has only 4 pages.

23. The remaining table has not been renumbered and so has the wrong caption number. To update it, select the caption and press <**F9**>.

i　*If more than one table, figure, etc. needs renumbering, select the whole document and press <**F9**>. All captions in the document will be renumbered.*

24. Save the document and leave it open.

Driving Lesson 43 - Creating a Table of Figures

▣ Park and Read

A table of figures is a list of the captions for pictures, charts, graphs, slides, or other illustrations in a document, along with the page numbers where they appear.

↱ Manoeuvres

1. Use the **Crossref** document for this exercise.

2. Place the cursor on page 1, beneath the list and the opening times reference.

3. Change the font to **Arial 12pt** bold, not italic. Type **Table of Figures** and press **<Enter>**.

4. From the **References** tab, select **Insert Table of Figures** from the **Captions** group. Select **Distinctive** from **Formats** and ensure the **Caption label** displays **Figure**.

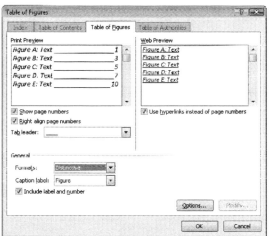

5. Click **OK**.

6. Use **<Ctrl>** and click to test the links.

7. Remove the caption from **Figure B**.

8. To renumber the remaining figures press **<Ctrl A>** then press **<F9>**.

9. To update the table, place the cursor in front of **Figure A** of the **Table of Figures**.

10. Press **<F9>** and select **Update entire table**.

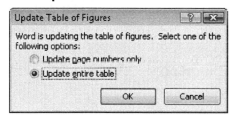

11. Click **OK**. Save the changes to the document and leave it open.

Driving Lesson 44 - Creating Index Entries

▣ Park and Read

An **index** shows the position of selected words or phrases in a document. Text required for inclusion in the index must be specifically marked before the index can be created.

Once styles and captions have been created in a document and cross-referencing and index entries have been marked, it is a simple process to create tables for the entries.

☞ Manoeuvres

1. Use **Crossref**. Highlight the first occurrence of the word **house** in the first paragraph.

2. From the **References** tab select **Mark Entry** from the **Index** group.

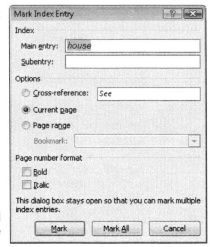

ℹ *To mark an index entry quickly, select the text and press <**Alt Shift X**>.*

ℹ *Indexes can also be marked by entering all the words to be indexed in a separate document. Save the document and from the **Index** group, select **Insert Index** and then **AutoMark**. Select the created file and Word will automatically index every occurrence of the word(s).*

3. Ensure **Current page** is selected from **Options**. Check **Italic** in **Page number format**.

4. Click **Mark All** to create an index entry for the first occurrence of **house** in each paragraph. The index entry is shown as a field, beginning with **XE**.

   Click the **Show/Hide** button, 🔣, if necessary to view the index entries.

   > year. The house{ XE "house" } is
   > al Elizabethan architecture in the

ℹ *Indexes are case sensitive: **House** is not the same as **house**.*

5. Click **Close** to remove the dialog box. Scroll through the document. An index mark appears next to every occurrence of **house**.

Driving Lesson 44 - Continued

6. Go to paragraph 2 on page 1 and highlight the word **gardens**.

7. Press <**Shift Alt X**> to view the **Mark Index Entry** dialog box.

8. Check **Italic** for **Page number format** then click **Mark All** and **Close** the dialog box.

9. Scroll down the document and create index entries for: **Elizabeth**, **tower**, **Pets' Corner**, **shop** and **tea room** (do not use the entries in the Table of figures or the paragraph titles).

10. On page 2 highlight the word **tower** and press <**Shift Alt X**>.

11. In the **Mark Index Entry** dialog box, select **Cross-reference** in the **Options** area and after **See**, type in **gardens**.

12. On page 3 highlight the word **maze** and press <**Shift Alt X**>.

13. In the **Mark Index Entry** dialog box, type **gardens** as the **Main entry** and **maze** as the **Subentry**.

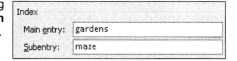

14. Save the document as **Index**.

15. To create the index, insert a page break at the end of the document and type **Index** on the new page. Format **Index** as **Heading 1**.

16. On a new line below this heading, from the **References** tab, select **Insert Index** [Insert Index] and display the **Index** tab in the dialog box.

17. Select the **Fancy** format. Click **OK** to create an **Index table**. Notice how **maze** is shown as a subentry of **gardens** and how the entry for **tower** shows **See gardens**. A cross reference has been created from the index.

18. Move to the first index entry **tea rooms** at the top of page 4 and if you don't see the **XE** fields, click **Show/Hide**, [¶].

19. To edit the index entry, change the text inside the quotation marks to **cafe**.

20. Select the index entry for **tower** in the text, select the entire field including the brackets **{ }**, and then press <**Delete**>.

21. To update the index to show the edited entry, click anywhere in the table and press <**F9**>.

22. Close the document, saving the changes.

Driving Lesson 45 - Revision: Referencing

This is not an ECDL test. Testing may only be carried out through certified ECDL test centres. This covers the features introduced in this section. Try not to refer to the preceding Driving Lessons while completing it.

1.   Open the document **Aurora Formatted**.

2.   Create endnotes in the **i,ii,iii** style for the following areas:

> **Greenland** page 1 paragraph 2 – **said by many to be the best place to view the lights**.

> **Eskimos** page 2 – **native Inuit people**.

3.   Move the insertion point back into the document. Amend the second endnote, adding the text **to give them their proper name**.

4.   Save the document as **Aurora Formatted2** and close it.

5.   Open **Stately Home Headings** and at the top of the document, create a table of contents based on the currently formatted headings.

6.   Insert a page break before **The Gardens** on page 1. Now update the table of contents.

7.   Create an index at the end of the document, using all headings as index marks.

8.   Save the document as **Stately Home3** and close it.

9.   Open the document **Predators** and create a bookmark for each heading in bold print.

10. Create an additional bookmark to the text **The grey nurse shark** in the **Methods of Reproduction** paragraph.

11. Insert a cross-reference from the first sentence of the **Diet** paragraph to the **The grey nurse shark** bookmark text.

12. Insert an appropriate graphic from **Clip Art** after the **Teeth** section and a second graphic after the **Sight** paragraph.

13. Apply captions **Figure 1**, **Figure 2** to the graphics.

14. Create a table of figures at the front of the document.

15. Save the document as **Jaws** and close it.

If you experienced any difficulty completing this Revision refer back to the Driving Lessons in this section. Then redo the Revision.

Once you are confident with the features, complete the Record of Achievement Matrix referring to the section at the end of the guide. Only when competent move on to the next Section.

Section 7
Collaborative Editing

By the end of this Section you should be able to:

Add and Remove Comments

Edit Comments

Track Changes to a Document

Accept or Reject Changes

Compare and Combine Documents

To gain an understanding of the above features, work through the **Driving Lessons** in this **Section**.

For each **Driving Lesson**, read the **Park and Read** instructions, without touching the keyboard, then work through the numbered steps of the **Manoeuvres** on the computer. Complete the **Revision Exercise(s)** at the end of the section to test your knowledge.

Driving Lesson 46 - Adding/Editing Comments

▣ Park and Read

Comments are used to make notes on a document. They are usually for on-screen reference but can be printed if required.

⟨ Manoeuvres

1. Open **Predators**.

2. In the first paragraph highlight the word **Mediterranean**. From the **Review** tab select **New Comment** from the **Comments** group.

3. In the **Comment** balloon at the right of the screen, enter **It has recently been discovered that the Great White Shark comes here to breed**. Click away from the comment area.

4. Brackets have been added to **Mediterranean** and a dashed line leads to the comment.

ℹ️ *Comment balloons are displayed by default in **Print** or **Web Layout View**. To remove the balloon option, select **Balloons** from the **Tracking** group and select **Show All Revisions Inline**. In **Draft View**, comments are entered in the **Reviewing** pane at the left or the bottom of the screen and the comment will appear as a caption when the mouse rests over the word in brackets.*

5. Find **cut** in the second paragraph and highlight it. Click the **New Comment** button and type **These cuts can result in shark attack**. Click away from the comment.

6. Highlight the word **Mediterranean** in the first paragraph. After a few seconds a note appears, with information about the comment.

ℹ️ *To hide comments from view, click the **Show Markup** drop down and uncheck **Comments**. Select the same option again to show them.*

7. Right click on the word **Mediterranean**. Select **Edit Comment** from the shortcut menu.

8. The cursor moves to the comment balloon. Edit the comment to **The Great White Shark uses the area as a nursery**. Click away from the comment.

9. Right click over the **cut** comment. Select **Delete Comment** from the shortcut menu to delete the comment.

10. Save the document as **Comments** and then close it.

Driving Lesson 47 - Tracking Changes

P Park and Read

When a document is being developed, particularly if it is being revised by different people, it is very useful to have all the amendments clearly visible within the document. By tracking changes to a document, it is possible to see where, when and who made the changes to it. Text that has been amended, added to or deleted from a document is shown.

Manoeuvres

1. Open the document **CiA**. This is a draft version of the document.

2. Select the **Review** tab and click **Track Changes**.

3. At the end of the first paragraph, enter **Although the company is based in the North East, products are sold throughout the world**.

4. Notice that the words have been coloured. This denotes that the text has been added to the document.

5. Delete **to meet the needs of the client** on the last line of the third paragraph. The text appears as strikethrough to show it has been deleted, unless the **Balloons** option is set to **Show Revisions in Balloons**, in which case the deleted text will appear in a balloon on the right.

6. Go to the end of the document.

7. Start a new paragraph and enter the following text: **For more information ring 0191 549 5002**.

8. Notice how all amended areas are noted by a vertical bar in the left margin.

9. Save the document as **Tracking** but do not close it.

Driving Lesson 48 - Accepting and Rejecting Changes

▣ Park and Read

Once changes have been tracked in a document, it is possible to view each change and either accept it or reject it. If the change is rejected, the text reverts to its original state. This is very useful when creating a joint report, or similar document.

A common scenario is for an author to create a report or similar document, then have it reviewed by one or more people. By tracking changes, the author can see which changes to the document have been suggested and decide whether to include them in the final version.

⌒ Manoeuvres

1.   Use **Tracking** for this lesson and click at the top of the document.

2.   Make sure the **Review** tab is visible.

3.   Click [🔲 Reviewing Pane ▾]. Notice that details of all changes are displayed in a reviewing pane at the bottom or the left of the screen. This includes data on which user made the change and when it was changed.

4.   Click **Next**, [⇒ Next] in the **Changes** group, to move to the first change.

5.   To accept the change, i.e. accept the added text, click **Accept**, [Accept ▾].

6.   The next change is highlighted. Accept this change.

7.   **Reject** the last change by clicking **Reject**, [Reject ▾]. The new text is removed.

8.   Notice that no text is now highlighted. This is because the changes have been either accepted or rejected.

9.   Click **OK** at the prompt.

10.   On the **Review** tab click **Reviewing Pane** to remove the pane and click the **Track Changes** button to revert to editing text normally.

11.   Save the document as **Final** before closing it.

Driving Lesson 49 - Compare and Combine

▣ Park and Read

When reviewed documents are returned, the amendments must be checked and incorporated into the original. Two documents, the original and the edited versions, can be compared, to identify any differences at a glance. Input from several reviewers can be merged then processed in one operation.

⌐ Manoeuvres

1. Assume for this exercise that you have sent copies of the original document, **Review**, to two colleagues for review, and they have returned the results as **R1** and **R2**.

2. Select the **Review** tab and click on **Compare**. Select **Combine** from the drop down menu.

3. Browse the supplied data files for an **Original document** and select **Review**.

4. Click in the **Revised document** box and browse the files, selecting **R1**.

5. Click on the **More** button [More >>] (if **Less** is showing, the box is already expanded). From **Show changes in** select **Original document**. Click **OK**. The changes are shown in a different colour.

6. Repeat these steps to compare and combine **R2**, combining with the original document.

7. Amendments from both reviewers are now included in one document, but are differentiated by colour from the original text. Move the pointer over the added text in the first paragraph of the combined document.

8. The first colour represents amendments from **Bob Browell**. Move the pointer over the added text in the second paragraph (shown in a different colour). The second colour represents amendments from **Bill Barnacle**.

9. From the **Tracking** group, select each option in turn from the **Display for Review** drop down list to see how the view of the document changes.

10. With the display **Final Showing Markup** selected, click the drop down arrow on the **Accept Change** button, and select **Accept All Changes in Document**. All tracking marks are removed. Save the file as **Reviewed**.

11. Assume the file is sent out for another review and has been returned. Compare and combine the document with **R3** into the original document.

12. Accept all the changes, then save the document as **Reviewed** again and close it. Close the **Review** document.

Driving Lesson 50 - Revision: Collaborative Editing

This is not an ECDL test. Testing may only be carried out through certified ECDL test centres. This covers the features introduced in this section. Try not to refer to the preceding Driving Lessons while completing it.

1. Open the document **Colorado**.

2. Set it up to track changes.

3. Insert a bold, centred **16pt** heading: **Colorado**.

4. Change the font size of the remainder of the text to **12pt**.

5. Make the first paragraph italic.

6. At the end of the final paragraph, enter **This natural wonder attracts hundreds of thousands of tourists annually**.

7. In the final paragraph, enter a comment after **marine sediment**, with the text **many fossils of sea creatures have been found**.

8. Work through the changes, accepting all apart from the inserted text, which should be rejected.

9. Close the document <u>without</u> saving.

10. Which feature allows you to see changes made to a reviewed document, within the original?

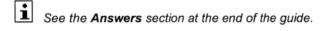 *See the **Answers** section at the end of the guide.*

If you experienced any difficulty completing this Revision refer back to the Driving Lessons in this section. Then redo the Revision.

Once you are confident with the features, complete the Record of Achievement Matrix referring to the section at the end of the guide. Only when competent move on to the next Section.

Section 8

Document Security

By the end of this Section you should be able to:

Password Protect a Document

Change Passwords

Remove Password Protection

To gain an understanding of the above features, work through the **Driving Lessons** in this **Section**.

For each **Driving Lesson**, read the **Park and Read** instructions, without touching the keyboard, then work through the numbered steps of the **Manoeuvres** on the computer. Complete the **Revision Exercise(s)** at the end of the section to test your knowledge.

Driving Lesson 51 - Password Protection

P Park and Read

Passwords can be assigned to certain documents to restrict access to them. This is particularly important if a computer is shared or is on a network where it can be accessed by other users.

Passwords can be used to control whether a document can be opened or modified. A document can also be protected, so that only tracked changes or comments may be added. Be careful, as without the password, access to the document will not be allowed; make sure to use a password that will not be forgotten.

Manoeuvres

1. Open the document **Articles**.

2. To add a password, select the **Office Button** then **Save As**. Click the **Tools** button from the dialog box and select **General Options**.

3. Locate **File encryption options for this document** and enter **stories** as the password in **Password to open**.

Driving Lesson 51 - Continued

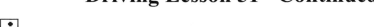

*To set a password to modify the document, enter it in the **File sharing options** area.*

4. Click **OK**. Re-enter the same password in the **Reenter password to open** box, click **OK** and save the document as **Password**.

5. Close the document.

6. Open the document **Password** using the password **stories** to check whether it worked. Close the document.

7. Open the document **Colorado**.

8. The content within a document can also be protected, select the **Review** tab and then **Protect Document**.

9. Select **Restrict Formatting and Editing** to display the appropriate task pane.

10. Check **2. Editing Restrictions** and from the drop down list, select **Comments**.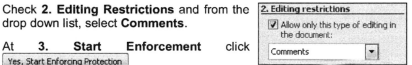

11. At **3. Start Enforcement** click Yes, Start Enforcing Protection.

12. At the **Start Enforcing Protection** dialog box, enter and re-enter the password **pass**. Click **OK**.

13. Save the document as **Locked**. This will allow a user to add comments, but not change the document in any other way.

14. Try to delete some text. You aren't able to because only the addition of comments is allowed.

15. Insert the comment **I can't change this** after the first paragraph.

16. To remove the protection, click **Stop Protection** in the task pane, enter the password **pass** and click **OK**. The document protection is removed. Try changing some text, there are no restrictions.

17. To add tracked changes protection from the **Editing Restrictions** drop down list, select **Tracked changes**.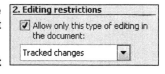

18. At **3. Start Enforcement** click **Yes, Start Enforcing Protection**.

19. Enter the password, **pass** and re-enter the password. Click **OK**.

20. Try changing some text, this will be allowed but it will automatically generate tracking.

21. Save the document using the same file name and then close it.

Driving Lesson 52 - Removing and Changing Passwords

Park and Read

If it is decided to change or remove a password, follow the same general steps as for adding a password. The original password is always required to access the document before any changes can be made, and the document must be saved after the password is changed.

Manoeuvres

1. Open the document **Password** using the password **stories**.

2. A rumour is circulating that the canteen workers have accessed the document. For security reasons, change to a different password using **Save As** then **Tools** and **General Options**.

3. In the **Password to open** area, enter a new password and click **OK**. Re-enter the password and click **OK**.

4. Save and then close the document.

5. Scandal is imminent - the document has been released to the press. Reopen the document and remove the password by deleting the contents in the **Password to open** box. Click **OK**.

6. Save the document and close it.

7. Check that the document is no longer password protected by reopening it.

8. Close the document.

9. Open the document **Locked**.

10. Display the **Restrict Formatting and Editing** task pane (if it is not already shown) by using the **Protect Document** button as before.

11. Click **Stop Protection**, enter the password, **pass** and click **OK**. This removes document protection. Close the task pane and then save the document with the same name.

12. Check that the document is no longer protected and can be edited by making a small change.

13. Save the document and then close it.

Passwords cannot be accidentally changed. They can only be changed when the document is open, which requires the password to be entered.

Driving Lesson 53 - Revision: Document Security

This is not an ECDL test. Testing may only be carried out through certified ECDL test centres. This covers the features introduced in this section. Try not to refer to the preceding Driving Lessons while completing it.

1. Open the document **Articles**.

2. Save the document as **Top Secret**, setting a password of **revision** that will be required to open it.

3. Close the document then test the password by opening it again.

4. Protect the document so that no changes may be made without the changes being tracked (**Tracked changes** option). Apply the password **secret** to this protection.

5. Test the protection by making changes to the document. They should be tracked.

6. Remove the document protection and the password.

7. Save the document using the same file name.

8. Close the document.

If you experienced any difficulty completing this Revision refer back to the Driving Lessons in this section. Then redo the Revision.

Once you are confident with the features, complete the Record of Achievement Matrix referring to the section at the end of the guide. Only when competent move on to the next Section.

Section 9
Master Documents &
Templates

By the end of this Section you should be able to:

Create a Master Document

Create a Subdocument

Add or Remove a Subdocument

Modify a Template

To gain an understanding of the above features, work through the **Driving Lessons** in this **Section**.

For each **Driving Lesson**, read the **Park and Read** instructions, without touching the keyboard, then work through the numbered steps of the **Manoeuvres** on the computer. Complete the **Revision Exercise(s)** at the end of the section to test your knowledge.

Driving Lesson 54 - Creating a Master Document

▣ Park and Read

A **master document** can be used when a report is too long to be maintained as one document. **Subdocuments** can be created, then inserted into the master document. They can be printed individually or altogether. They can also be used to create tables of contents. Master documents can be used in **Outline View** to organise headings, contents and indexes.

An example of a master document/subdocument structure could be a book, where the master document contains the title and the chapter headings, and each individual chapter is in a separate subdocument.

☞ Manoeuvres

1. ˉ Start a new document and switch to **Outline** view.

2. Notice the **Master Document** group at the right of the **Outlining** tab.

3. With the style as **Level 1**, enter the title **The Book I Always Wanted to Write**.

4. Press <**Enter**>.

5. Change the level of the next line to **Level 2**.

6. Type in the text **Chapter One**. The **Master Document** is now ready to have subdocuments added.

7. Leave the document open and move to the next Driving Lesson.

Driving Lesson 55 - Creating a Subdocument

▣ Park and Read

A **subdocument** is created and saved in the same way as a normal document. Once a subdocument is inserted/created in a master document, the two documents are linked. This allows the subdocument to be opened and changed individually, or through the master document. A master document can also help members of a workgroup to create and update parts of a long document.

⇪ Manoeuvres

1. With the insertion point still at the end of the **Chapter One** text, click the **Show Document** button and click **Create**. This places the chapter heading inside a grey outline, defining the subdocument.

2. Save the document as **My Book**. The subdocument will automatically be saved as **Chapter One**.

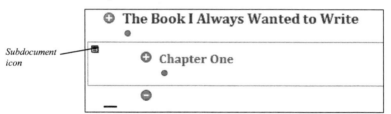

Subdocument icon

3. Double click on the subdocument icon to open **Chapter One**. Underneath the title enter **I was born in the early summer of 19##**. Click **Save**.

4. Using the **Taskbar**, switch back to **My Book** to view the reflected changes. Close both documents, saving if prompted.

5. Open **My Book**. Note how the subdocument is now displayed only as a link to a file name, e.g.

> C:\Documents and Settings\Dawn\My Documents\CIA DATA FILES\Advanced ECDL\AM3 Word 2007 Data\Chapter One.docx

6. Move the pointer over the file name, hold down **<Ctrl>** and click once on the file name to open the document.

7. Close it again. Click at the end of the **Chapter One** file name. Click **Expand Subdocuments**. All of the entered text is now displayed. Text can also be entered here.

Driving Lesson 55 - Continued

8. Click beside the last text entry icon ◉ and enter **Chapter Two**. Make this a subdocument by clicking .

9. Save **My Book**.

10. Double click on **Chapter Two**'s subdocument icon and enter the text **I went to school at…**. Save and close and **Chapter Two**.

11. Collapse the subdocuments using the **Collapse Subdocuments** button. The **Master Document** appears similar to that below.

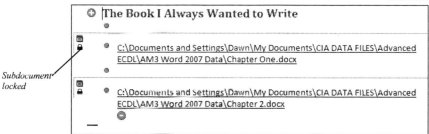

Subdocument locked

12. Subdocuments are usually **locked** when they are not to be modified, i.e. are read-only. However, in this case, expand the documents and the locks will be opened.

13. Click **Show Document**, to view where the **Section Breaks** (dotted lines) occur. Note that they are before and after each subdocument. **Section Breaks** were covered in a previous Driving Lesson.

14. Click on **Show Document** again.

15. **Print Preview** the **Master Document**.

16. Close **Print Preview**, but leave **My Book** open.

Driving Lesson 56 - Adding and Removing a Subdocument

Park and Read

Previously created documents can be used as subdocuments.

Manoeuvres

1. Use the master document **My Book**, which should still be open from the previous Driving Lesson.

2. Click beside the last text entry icon ⊖ and click the **Insert Subdocument** button, 🔲 Insert.

3. From the data files, select the document **Chapter 3** and click **Open**.

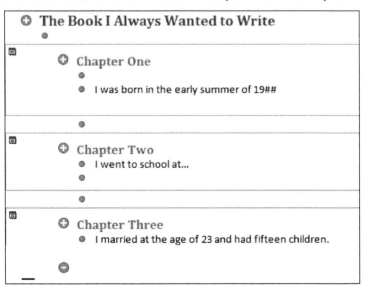

4. The document is inserted as a subdocument.

5. To delete the **Chapter 3** subdocument, first make sure the subdocuments are expanded.

6. Click on the **Chapter 3** subdocument icon and press **<Delete>** to remove it.

7. Save and close **My Book**.

Driving Lesson 57 - Modifying a Template

▣ Park and Read

A template is a special document that is used as the basis for creating other documents. It contains the necessary formatting and framework to ensure that all documents created from it are consistent in appearance. It is possible to change a template as desired after it has been created, in the same way as normal documents can be edited.

⌓ Manoeuvres

1.   Open the document **CV**. Select **Save As** and change the **File name** to **CV template** and the **Save as type** to **Word Template**.   Change the **Location** to **Templates**. Click **Save**.

2.   To apply a watermark, select the **Page Layout** tab and click the **Watermark** button, then select **Custom Watermark**.

3.   Select **Text watermark** and in the **Text** box enter **Template**.

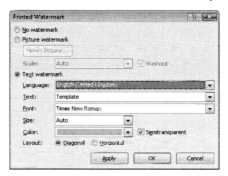

4.   Click **OK**.

5.   Select all of the text in the document. Change the font to **Book Antiqua**, or an alternative if this font is unavailable.

6.   Select **Save As**. In the **Save As** dialog box, use the same file name **CV template**. The location is the **Templates** folder and the **Save as type** is **Word Template**.

7.   Click **Save**. Close the template.

8.   To delete a template from the **Templates** folder, click the **Office Button**, select **New** and click **My templates**.

9.   Right click on the **CV template** icon. Select **Delete** from the menu.

10.   Select **Yes** at the prompt and click **Cancel** to close the **New** dialog box. Cancel the **New Document** window.

Driving Lesson 58 - Revision: Master Documents and Templates

This is not an ECDL test. Testing may only be carried out through certified ECDL test centres. This covers the features introduced in this section. Try not to refer to the preceding Driving Lessons while completing it.

1. Create a master document from the following files: **Beverages**, **Cuisine** and **Deli**.

2. Remove any unwanted blank pages.

3. Save the master document as **Food and drink**.

4. Preview the master document then adjust the section breaks so that there are only three pages (you may need to switch views to do this).

5. Remove the subdocument **Deli**.

6. Save the changes to the master document.

7. Close it.

8. Open one of the prepared templates (in **Installed Templates**) - the **Equity Fax** as a template.

9. Add a text watermark (**CONFIDENTIAL**).

10. Save the amended template as **Watermarked Fax.dotx** in the template location.

11. Delete the amended template.

If you experienced any difficulty completing this Revision refer back to the Driving Lessons in this section. Then redo the Revision.

Once you are confident with the features, complete the Record of Achievement Matrix referring to the section at the end of the guide. Only when competent move on to the next Section.

Section 10

Field Codes and

Forms

By the end of this Section you should be able to:

Insert, Delete, Edit and Update Field Codes

Lock or Unlock a Field

Create and Edit a Form

Change Form Field Options

Protect and Delete Form Fields

To gain an understanding of the above features, work through the **Driving Lessons** in this **Section**.

For each **Driving Lesson**, read the **Park and Read** instructions, without touching the keyboard, then work through the numbered steps of the **Manoeuvres** on the computer. Complete the **Revision Exercise(s)** at the end of the section to test your knowledge.

Driving Lesson 59 - Working with Field Codes

▣ Park and Read

Fields are used for two main purposes. Firstly to insert codes, which are then substituted with current information such as the date or the document title. Secondly, to define parts of a document which will accept data input, in a form for example. Form fields are described in a later Driving Lesson.

Manoeuvres

1.　Open the document **Summary**.

2.　Click the **Office Button** and select **Prepare**, then **Properties**. Add your name to the document as **Author** and **Technical Report** as the **Title**. Close the **Document Properties Panel**.

3.　Add four blank lines to the top of the document. Click in the first blank line and select the **Insert** tab. Click ▣ Quick Parts ▾ and then click **Field** from the drop down list. The **Field** dialog box is displayed.

4.　From the **Categories**, select **Document Information** and then select **Title** from **Field names**. Click **OK**.

> **ⓘ** *If a field code {TITLE...} is shown instead of the field content (Technical Report), press <Alt F9> to switch the view.*

5.　On the second line insert the field **Author**, and on the third line insert the field **FileSize**. Both fields are from **Document Information**.

6.　On the fourth line insert the field **Fill-in**, from the **Mail Merge** category. Specify a prompt of **Enter text**. Click **OK**, enter **Information** and click **OK**.

> **ⓘ** *Fill-in fields prompt for data to be entered whenever the field is updated. These are often used in templates and in mail merge applications.*

7.　Fields can be added to **Headers and Footers**. From the **Insert** tab select **Header** then **Edit Header**.

8.　Click **Quick Parts,** select the **FileName** field, check **Add path to filename** and click **OK** to add the **file name and path** field to the header.

9.　Click **Go To Footer,** click the **Date and Time** button and insert the time as a field. With **Update automatically** checked, click **OK**.

10.　Tab to the right of the **Footer** and insert the current date using the **Date and Time** button.

11.　Click the **Close Header and Footer** button.

12.　Print a copy of the document.

13.　Save the document as **Fields** and close it.

Driving Lesson 60 - Editing and Updating Field Codes

P Park and Read

Some fields containing numerical information, for example the date or time, are updated automatically when printing, previewing or merging. Other fields are not. All fields can however be updated manually at any time by using the <**F9**> function key.

Manoeuvres

1. Open the document **Time**. Each of the four numbered lines contains a time field.

2. Use <**Alt F9**> if necessary make sure the time values are being shown rather than the field codes. Notice each value has a different format.

3. Press <**Alt F9**> to view the field codes. Notice that each field was given a different format definition when it was inserted.

4. Press <**Alt F9**> again to view the time values. Notice they are not current, time has passed since the document was opened.

5. To update a single field, the cursor must be within the field. Position the cursor inside the time field in line 1. Press <**F9**> to update the time.

6. Field codes themselves may be edited. Right click in the field on line 1.

7. Select **Edit Field** from the shortcut menu. The **Field** dialog box is displayed.

8. From **Time** select from the **Field names** list and choose an **am/pm** format.

9. Click **OK**. The field now shows the current time in the chosen format.

10. Note all the time values which are displayed, then print out a single copy of the document. All dates and times are automatically updated on printing, except for line 3 which is locked (see next Driving Lesson).

11. Leave the document open for the next Driving Lesson.

Driving Lesson 61 - Locking/Unlocking Fields

▣ Park and Read

Sometimes fields may need to be fixed, i.e. not require updating. In order to fix a specific value in a field, the **Lock Field** key <**Ctrl F11**> is used.

⌐ Manoeuvres

1. Use the document **Time** for this Driving Lesson.

2. Wait for a minute then use <**F9**> to update the time in line 2.

3. Try using the same process to update the time on the line 3. This field has been locked; the time is fixed and will not be updated.

4. With the cursor still in the field on line 3, unlock the field by pressing <**Ctrl Shift F11**>.

5. Now use <**F9**> and the time will update successfully.

6. Highlight the time in line 4. Lock the field by pressing <**Ctrl F11**>.

7. Try updating the field using <**F9**>.

8. Now unlock the field by pressing <**Ctrl Shift F11**>. Use <**F9**> to update.

9. Field codes can be deleted easily. Select the time field in line 4, using double click or click and drag to make sure the entire field is highlighted.

10. Press <**Delete**>. The field is removed.

ℹ️ *Fields can be deleted in either view, **Field code** or **Field content**.*

11. Close the document <u>without</u> saving.

Driving Lesson 62 - Creating and Editing Forms

🅿 Park and Read

Form Fields are created to enable data to be entered into a document, which is then called a form. They are special fields that will prompt for data entry when the form is displayed. The layout of the form is designed first, then the fields are created. The form must be protected before the fields will work.

🖐 Manoeuvres

1. Before you can work with a form, *Word* must be set up to create forms. If the **Developer** tab is not displayed on the **Ribbon**, click the **Office Button** and select **Word Options**. Click **Popular**, check **Show Developer tab in the Ribbon** and click **OK**.

2. Start a new document and enter the text as below:

    Memo

    To:
    From:
    Date:
    Subject:
    Urgent:

    Message:

3. Select all of the text and insert a left tab stop at **3cm**. Position the cursor after **To:** and press **<Tab>** to move to the tab stop.

4. Select the **Developer** tab to display the **Controls** group.

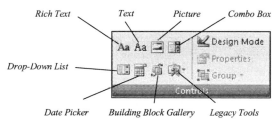

5. Click **Legacy Tools** and click once on **Drop Down Form Field**, 🔲, to create a field.

6. To delete the field, place the cursor in front of it; press **<Delete>** once to highlight the field, then again to delete it.

7. Now create the **Drop Down List** again, as it is needed for this form and leave the document open for the next Driving Lesson.

Driving Lesson 63 - Form Field Options

▣ Park and Read

After a form field has been created, various options can be set to define the operation of the field, using form field options. For a **Drop-Down Form Field** for example, the choices given within the field have to be supplied. For a **Text Form Field**, the options include the type and format of entered data.

⟲ Manoeuvres

1. Using the document from the previous Driving Lesson, keep the cursor in the field and click the **Properties** button, [⌖ Properties].

2. In **Drop-down item**, enter **Andrew Simpson**. Click **Add**.

3. Enter the following names in the same manner: **Susan Peters**, **Ishmael Rampuri** and **Gita Patel**. Click **OK** to close the dialog box.

4. Click after **From** and press **<Tab>**. Click on **Legacy Tools** and select **Text Form Field**, [abl], from the **Legacy Forms** section to create a field. Click [⌖ Properties] to display the options for the field and in **Default text**, enter your name and click **OK**.

5. Similarly create another **Text Form Field** after **Date**. Click [⌖ Properties] to define options for this field.

6. From **Type**, select **Current date** and in the **Date format** box, select a format of **dd MMMM yyyy**. Click **OK**.

7. Place another **Text Form Field** after **Subject**.

8. Click after **Urgent**, press **<Tab>**, then click on **Legacy Tools** and select **Check Box Form Field**, [☑], from the **Legacy Forms** section.

9. Finally, create a **Text Form Field** on the line below **Message**.

Driving Lesson 63 - Continued

10.　Define options for this field - click **Add Help Text**. Complete the box on the **Status Bar** tab as shown in the diagram. This text will appear on the **Status Bar** when the text field is entered.

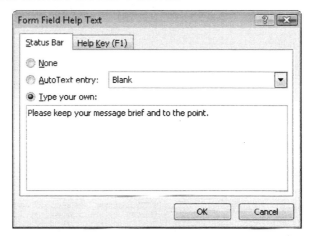

11.　Select the **Help Key (F1)** tab. Select **Type your own** and enter **Don't ramble on!** This text will appear if <**F1**> is pressed when in the **Message** field.

12.　Click **OK** and then **OK** again.

13.　Press <**Alt F9**> to view the field codes, then again to see the field content.

14.　Leave the document open for the next Driving Lesson.

Driving Lesson 64 - Protecting Form Fields

▣ Park and Read

To allow the **Form Fields** to work on a form, the document must be protected. Once protected, data can only be entered in the **Form Fields**; no other changes will be allowed to the document.

☞ Manoeuvres

1. Using the document from the previous Driving Lesson, make sure the field content is shown (not field codes) and click the **Protect Document** button.

2. Select the **Restrict Formatting and Editing** option to display the relevant pane. Check option **2. Editing Restrictions** in the pane and select **Filling in forms** from the drop down list.

3. In option **3**, click **Yes, Start Enforcing Protection**. Click **OK** at the dialog box without entering a password. The document is protected. Nothing can be changed in the document apart from the content of the form fields. Save the document as **Form**.

4. Click in the first field - a drop down arrow appears. Choose a name, then press <**Tab**> to move to the next field.

5. Your name is entered here already. Press <**Tab**> to move to the **Subject**. Notice the current date is automatically set and cannot be changed.

6. In **Subject**, enter **Important Notice** then press <**Tab**>.

7. Click once in the field box next to **Urgent** to set the option.

8. Press <**Tab**> look at the **Status Bar** to see the **Help Text**. Press <**F1**>.

9. Click **OK** and enter the following message: **Please note that the budget has been cut by 10%, therefore I will need new costings urgently**.

10. Try to change the word **Message** to **Comment**. It will not be allowed.

11. Press <**Alt F9**> to view the field codes. This will not be allowed.

12. Print the document, then save it as **Form2**.

13. Remove the protection by clicking the **Stop Protection** in the task pane.

14. Press <**Alt F9**> to view the field codes. Select the whole of the field **{FORMCHECKBOX}** and press <**Delete**> to remove it.

15. Close the document.

Driving Lesson 65 - Revision: Fields and Forms

This is not an ECDL test. Testing may only be carried out through certified ECDL test centres. This covers the features introduced in this section. Try not to refer to the preceding Driving Lessons while completing it.

1.　Open the document **Shark**. Display the **Document Properties Panel** and make sure **Title**, **Subject** and **Author** are entered. Add them if necessary.

2.　Use fields to insert the **Title** and **Author** on new lines immediately under the heading. Right align the fields.

3.　On a new line at the end of the document, type **Report created at** and insert a date field.

4.　Print the document.

5.　Change the **Author** details in file properties to a different name and update the **Author** field in the document to reflect the change.

6.　Change the **Title** field so that it shows the **Filename** instead.

7.　Lock the **Report created at** field so that it will never be updated.

8.　Print the document again, save it as **Shark74**, and then close it

9.　Start a new document to create a form inviting four colleagues to a meeting. Enter the text as below:

> **Meeting Schedule**
> **To:**
> **From:**
> **Date:**
> **Time:**
> **Agenda:**
> **Reply req?**

10.　Set a tab at **4cm** for all of the text, then click after **To:** and press <Tab>. Insert a **Drop-Down Form** field and enter the names of four colleagues (don't forget to use the **Form Field Options**).

11.　Create **Text Form** fields for **From: Date: Time:** and **Agenda:**.

12.　Create a **Check Box Form** field after **Reply req?** and **Protect the form**.

13.　Select a name from the list for **To:**, enter your name in **From:**, enter today's date and the time as the current time. Check the check box.

14.　Save the document as **Meeting** and close it. Close the **Forms** task pane.

If you experienced any difficulty completing this Revision refer back to the Driving Lessons in this section. Then redo the Revision.

Once you are confident with the features, complete the Record of Achievement Matrix referring to the section at the end of the guide. Only when competent move on to the next Section.

Section 11
Mail Merge

By the end of this Section you should be able to:

Edit a Mail Merge Data Source

Sort and Query a Data Source

Use Ask and IF Fields

Use Different Data Sources

To gain an understanding of the above features, work through the **Driving Lessons** in this **Section**.

For each **Driving Lesson**, read the **Park and Read** instructions, without touching the keyboard, then work through the numbered steps of the **Manoeuvres** on the computer. Complete the **Revision Exercise(s)** at the end of the section to test your knowledge.

Driving Lesson 66 - Editing a Data Source

🅿 Park and Read

Often the same **Data Source** will be used with any number of **Main Documents** over a period of time, so it must be well planned and kept up to date. For example, a mailing list data source will have to be edited when contact details or addresses are changed.

⤵ Manoeuvres

1. Start a new, blank document, view the **Mailings** tab, choose **Start Mail Merge** and select the **Step by Step Mail Merge Wizard**.

2. Read and accept the defaults on Steps **1** and **2** and move to **Step 3 of 6** in the **Task Pane**. Click on **Browse** and locate the supplied data files.

3. Select the **Clients** address list and click **Open**. The **Mail Merge Recipients** dialog box is displayed.

4. To edit the list, click on the data source **Clients.accdb** in the lower left of the dialog box and click the **Edit** button. The **Edit Data Source** dialog box is displayed.

5. **Freda Jones**, the first person on the list, has left the country. Select Freda's record in the **Edit Data Source** dialog box and click **Delete Entry** and then **Yes** at the prompt.

6. Use the dialog box to locate the record for **BB Computer Consultants**. They have moved to **49 George Street**. Amend the record accordingly. Click **OK** to close the dialog box and click **Yes** to update the recipient list.

7. Click **OK** to close the **Mail Merge Recipients** dialog box then close the document <u>without</u> saving.

8. Now open the document **Invitation**, which already has a data source, **Contacts**, linked to it. Click **Yes** when prompted to continue. From the **Select Data Source** dialog box, locate the supplied data folder, select the **Contacts** data source, and click **Open**.

9. View the **Step by Step Mail Merge Wizard** and display step **3**. Click the **Edit Recipient List** button.

10. **George Murphy** has asked to be removed from the mailing list. Select **Contacts.accdb** in the lower left of the dialog box and click **Edit**. Select George Murphy's record, click **Delete Entry** and select **Yes** at the prompt.

11. Now click **OK** and then **Yes** to save the changes and return to the **Mail Merge Recipients** box. George Murphy's record has been removed.

12. Leave the **Mail Merge Recipients** dialog box open.

Driving Lesson 67 - Sorting a Data Source

Park and Read

It is possible to sort the records in a data source in ascending or descending alphabetical or numerical order. A data source can also be queried, so that only selected records are used in the mail merge, for example to send letters only to people in a particular city.

Manoeuvres

1. Make sure the **Mail Merge Recipients** dialog box is open.

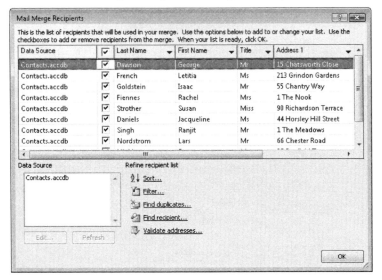

2. To sort the data alphabetically by surname, click the **Last Name** heading.

3. Notice how the records are now sorted in alphabetical order.

Driving Lesson 67 - Continued

4. To sort the records in descending alphabetical order of surname, click again on the **Last Name** header.

Data Source	☑	Last Name ▼	First Name ▼	Title ▼	Address 1 ▼
Contacts.accdb	☑	Strother	Susan	Miss	90 Richardson Terrace
Contacts.accdb	☑	Smith	Elaine	Miss	58 Orpington Close
Contacts.accdb	☑	Singh	Ranjit	Mr	1 The Meadows
Contacts.accdb	☑	Nordstrom	Lars	Mr	66 Chester Road
Contacts.accdb	☑	Hipkiss	Dawn	Mrs	25 Benfield Terrace
Contacts.accdb	☑	Goldstein	Isaac	Mr	55 Chantry Way
Contacts.accdb	☑	French	Letitia	Ms	213 Grindon Gardens
Contacts.accdb	☑	Fiennes	Rachel	Mrs	1 The Nook
Contacts.accdb	☑	Dawson	George	Mr	15 Chatsworth Close
Contacts.accdb	☑	Daniels	Jacqueline	Ms	44 Horsley Hill Street

5. To **query** this data source and send letters to people living in **Sunderland**, but not to the others, use the scroll bar at the bottom of the **Mail Merge Recipients** dialog box to view the **City** heading.

6. Make sure data in the **City** column is fully displayed. Click the drop down arrow on the **City** heading.

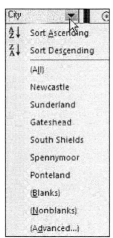

7. Select **Sunderland** from the list. The arrow changes to blue to indicate that the list has been filtered. Click **OK**.

8. View the **Mail Merge Task Pane** and move to **Step 5 of 6** to preview the letters.

9. Move through the three letters using the **Task Pane** to see that they all live in **Sunderland**.

10. Leave **Invitation** open.

Driving Lesson 68 - Using Different Data Sources

▣ Park and Read

The data source used in a mail merge can be changed to a different source. The main document may have to be changed to match the new source.

⌐ Manoeuvres

1. Use the main document **Invitation** for this Driving Lesson. Your colleague in Marketing has given you an address list containing new customers, to whom you want to send an invitation to the company's open day.

2. View the **Mail Merge Wizard** at **Step 3 of 6**.

3. From the **Use an existing list** area of the **Wizard**, click **Select a different list**.

4. Make sure **All Data Sources** is displayed in the dialog box, and locate the data files.

5. Select the **Clients** database and click **Open**. The list of contacts is displayed in the **Mail Merge Recipients** dialog box.

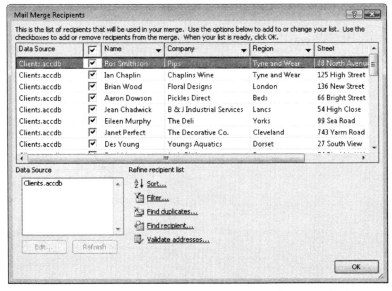

6. Click **OK**. Now the main document has to be edited to contain the correct merge fields.

Driving Lesson 68 - Continued

7. Delete the existing merge fields in the document.

8. Click on the **Insert Merge Field** button on the **Mail Merge** tab to reveal the list of available fields in the *Access* table.

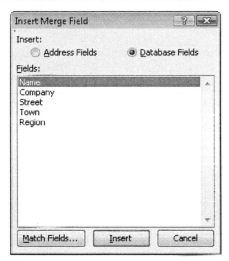

9. **Insert** the new fields into the main document so that they match the diagram below (you can use the list available from the bottom half of the **Insert Merge Field** button to insert the fields without displaying the dialog box).

10. Close the **Insert Merge Field** dialog box, if open. Adjust the spacing appropriately.

11. Move to **Step 5** on the **Task Pane** and preview the document to be merged (use the double chevrons to move forward and back), which should contain 30 letters.

12. Move to **Step 6 Complete the merge**.

13. Click **Edit individual letters** and to save the merged file, select to merge **All** records and click **OK**.

14. Save the merged file as **Updatemerge** and then close it.

15. Close **Invitation** without saving.

Driving Lesson 69 - Ask and IF Fields

Park and Read

Various special fields can be added to a mail merge main document in certain situations. For example, if a recipient lives in area A, send a letter with a money off coupon attached; if they live in area B, send just the letter. An **IF...then...else** field would be used to do this. If an **ASK** field is used in a mail merge main document, a prompt is displayed each time you merge a new data record. For example, to enter a date that will change every month, like a meeting or event. **Ask** must be used in conjunction with a **Ref** field to allow the results of the query to be displayed.

Manoeuvres

1. Open the document **Showroom** (linked to the data source **Customer List.accdb** in the same location).

2. This is a letter from a car showroom to promote new models to existing customers. Depending on their home address, they are invited to attend one of two possible locations.

3. Place the cursor between **to** and **on** and ensure the **Mailings** tab is displayed.

4. Click **Rules** ⌜🔲 Rules ▾⌝ from the **Write and Insert Fields** group and select **If...Then...Else**.

5. From **Field name** select **City** and ensure **Comparison** shows **Equal to**. Enter **Sunderland** in **Compare to**.

6. In **Insert this text**, type **Park Lane Showroom** and in **Otherwise insert this text**, type **North Road Showroom**.

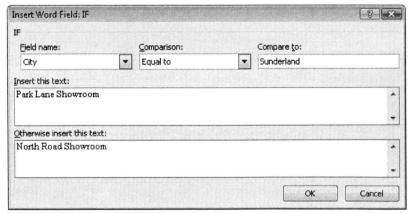

Driving Lesson 69 - Continued

7. Click **OK**. This means that any customers living in Sunderland will be invited to Park Lane Showroom, but those in Newcastle will be invited to North Road Showroom. The field can be formatted. Highlight the field text and change the font to **Arial** to match the other text.

8. View the **Mailings** tab again and complete the merge (**Edit individual documents**), merging all and saving the merge file as **Carmerge**.

9. Review the letters to see the **IF** field in action.

10. Close any open documents, saving the changes to **Showroom**.

11. Open the document **Event**, linked to the data source **Visitors.accdb**.

12. This mail merge will contain a date that varies. An **Ask** field needs to be used. As these fields work via bookmarks, one needs to be created where the field information is to be shown.

13. Click between **on** and **and** in paragraph 2 and select the **Insert** tab and then **Bookmark**.

14. Enter the **Bookmark name** as **Event_Date** and click **Add**.

15. Click in front of **As one of our...** and from the **Mailings** tab, select **Rules** and then **Ask**.

ℹ️ *The location of the **Ask** field is not important, as it will not be seen in the finished document, but it must be before the first bookmark.*

16. Select the **Event_Date** bookmark and in **Prompt** type **Enter the date of the next garden party**.

17. In **Default bookmark text**, type **the last Thursday of this month**. This will be added if the user doesn't type anything else. Check **Ask once** so that all the letters have the same response.

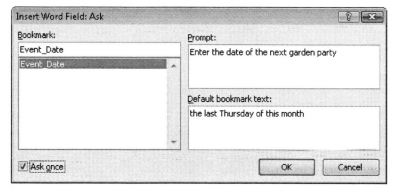

Driving Lesson 69 - Continued

18. Click **OK** then **OK** again. The result does not appear until a **Ref** field has been added.

19. Position the cursor at the bookmark location and select the **Insert** tab. From **Quick Parts** in the **Text** group, select **Field** to display the **Field** dialog box.

20. Change the **Category** to **Links and References** and select **Ref** from the list.

21. From **Bookmark** name, select **Event_Date** and from the **Format** drop down select **Title case**.

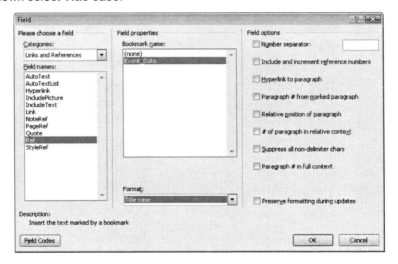

22. Click **OK**.

23. Use the **Mailings** tab to complete the merge. The prompt will appear before the final letters are printed or edited.

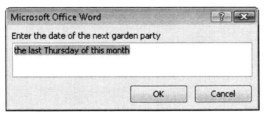

24. Type in **27th july** and click **OK**. The date is added to the letters. Check all the letters for the **Title case** date **27th July**.

25. Close any documents <u>without</u> saving.

Driving Lesson 70 - Revision: Mail Merge

This is not an ECDL test. Testing may only be carried out through certified ECDL test centres. This covers the features introduced in this section. Try not to refer to the preceding Driving Lessons while completing it.

1. Open the document **Conference**. This is a prepared mail merge letter, linked to a data source named **Clients**.

2. Locate the **Clients** data source from the files supplied and use the **Edit Recipient List** button, , to view the data form.

3. Change Aaron Dowson's company name to **Direct Pickles**.

4. In the **Mail Merge Recipients** dialog box, sort the records alphabetically by name.

5. Close **Conference** <u>without</u> saving.

6. Open **Conference** again.

7. To open a new data source – an *Access* database, select the **Conferences** database from the **Select Data Source** dialog box and the **No training** query from the **Select Table** dialog box.

8. Edit the main document, **Conference**, removing the original merge fields.

9. Insert the following fields in suitable positions:

    First Name

    Last Name

    Company

    Address1

    Address2

    City

10. Print the merged document.

11. Close **Conference** <u>without</u> saving.

If you experienced any difficulty completing this Revision refer back to the Driving Lessons in this section. Then redo the Revision.

Once you are confident with the features, complete the Record of Achievement Matrix referring to the section at the end of the guide. Only when competent move on to the next Section.

Section 12

Linking and

Embedding

By the end of this Section you should be able to:

Link Data into a Document

Update and Break Links

Embed Data

Modify Embedded Data

To gain an understanding of the above features, work through the **Driving Lessons** in this **Section**.

For each **Driving Lesson**, read the **Park and Read** instructions, without touching the keyboard, then work through the numbered steps of the **Manoeuvres** on the computer. Complete the **Revision Exercise(s)** at the end of the section to test your knowledge.

Driving Lesson 71 - Linking Data

▣ Park and Read

Documents can be **linked** to external data from a variety of other applications. Linking an object means that if its source data is changed, those changes can be reflected in the object. It also means that the source data can be opened directly from *Word*. Text from other documents, data and charts from spreadsheets can all be linked.

⌒ Manoeuvres

1. Start a new document and give it the heading **Puppy Facts**, **Arial**, **16pt**, **bold**, **centred**.

2. Text from another document is to be linked to this one. Position the cursor under the title and select the **Insert** tab. Select the **Object** drop down arrow from the **Text** group and then **Object**.

3. From the **Object** dialog box, select **Create from File**. **Browse** the data and select the **Puppy Info** document. Click **Insert**.

4. To ensure the file is linked, click on **Link to file**. Also click on **Display as icon** to see the effect.

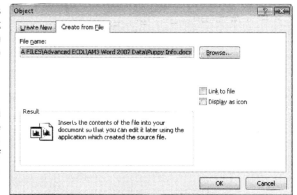

5. Click **OK**.

6. On a new line, a chart is to be Inserted, showing numbers of registered breeders. Start a new line.

7. From the **Insert** tab, select **Object** then **Object** again. At the dialog box, select the **Create from File** tab.

8. Browse for the file **Pups.xlsx**. Check **Link to file** but do not check **Display as icon**. Click **OK**.

9. Reduce the size of the linked chart to between the margins of the page.

10. Save the document as **Puppy Facts** and close it.

Driving Lesson 72 - Updating Links

▣ Park and Read

Whenever a document containing links is opened, you will always be prompted to update the links. If the option is accepted, all linked objects within the document will be updated with the current versions from the source data. If not, they will be left unchanged.

☞ Manoeuvres

1. Open the source file **Puppy Info**.

2. Delete the word **Labrador** in the first line and save and close the file.

3. Open the *Excel* file **Pups**.

4. Select the **Breeder Data** tab, if not already selected.

5. Change the value for **East** to **179**.

6. Select the **Breeder Ratios** tab to see the change.

7. Save and close the file. Close *Excel*.

8. Open the **Puppy Facts** document containing the links. The following prompt appears.

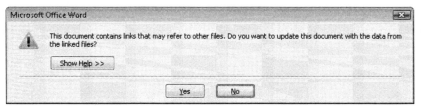

9. Select **Yes** to update the links. Notice the figure on the pie chart for **East** has changed to **179**.

10. Double click on the icon to open the linked *Word* document. The word **Labrador** is missing from the first line.

11. Close the **Puppy Info** document.

12. To break the link to the chart, select the **Office Button**, then from **Prepare**, select **Edit Links to Files**.

Driving Lesson 72 - Continued

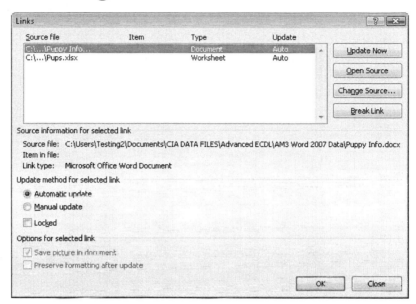

13. From the list, select the **Pups.xlsx** file and click **Break Link**.

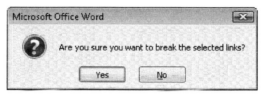

14. Select **Yes** at the prompt.

15. Click **OK** to close the **Links** dialog box.

16. Save and close **Puppy Facts**.

17. In *Excel* open **Pups** again and change the figure for **West** to **350** (**Breeder Data** tab). Check on the **Breeder Ratios** tab that the chart has been updated.

18. Save and close the file.

19. Reopen **Puppy Facts**, updating when prompted.

20. Notice that the figure for **West** remains at **238**, because the link has been broken.

21. Save the changes to **Puppy Facts** and leave it open.

Driving Lesson 73 - Embedding Data

▣ Park and Read

When an object is **embedded** in a document, it will <u>not</u> change if the source file is amended. The default for inserting or pasting objects into a document is for them to be embedded. A linked object will be changed to an embedded object if the link is broken.

Manoeuvres

1.   Using **Puppy Facts**, place the cursor beneath the pie chart.

2.   In *Excel* open **Pups** and select the **Litters** tab. Save and close the file.

3.   In **Puppy Facts**, select the **Insert** tab, then **Object** and **Object** again. From **Create from File** browse and select **Pups.xlsx**.

4.   Do <u>not</u> check **Link to file**.

5.   Insert the file and resize it ensuring it is fully displayed.

ⓘ *You may need to use **Worksheet Edit** from the shortcut menu to resize the object.*

6.   Use the **Office Button** to view the **Links**. The chart is not shown, because it is embedded rather than linked.

ⓘ *If you copy a chart from Excel and paste it into a Word document it will also be embedded. However, you will not be able to edit the chart using this method. See next Driving Lesson.*

7.   Save the changes to the document and leave it open.

Driving Lesson 74 - Modifying Embedded Data

▣ Park and Read

Embedded data can be updated manually from within *Word*. By double clicking on the embedded object, an editing mode is started, which allows you to make changes.

☞ Manoeuvres

1. Double click on the embedded chart, **Litter Size Comparison** to activate the editing mode.

2. Click in cell **D4** and change the figure for **Ebony**'s **2002** litter to **10**.

3. Press **<Enter>**. Notice the figure and the chart have been updated.

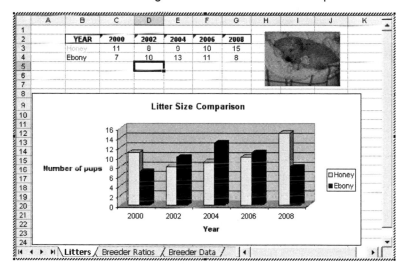

4. Click on the document area, away from the spreadsheet extract, to exit edit mode.

ℹ️ *The original chart in **Pups** has not been affected as this was embedded and not linked.*

5. Save the changes to the document and close it.

6. Click on the embedded worksheet and with the handles displayed, press **<Delete>** to remove the embedded data.

7. Close the document <u>without</u> saving.

8. Close *Excel*.

Driving Lesson 75 - Revision: Linking and Embedding

This is not an ECDL test. Testing may only be carried out through certified ECDL test centres. This covers the features introduced in this section. Try not to refer to the preceding Driving Lessons while completing it.

1. Start a new document and link the *Excel* worksheet **Sales**.

2. Resize the linked object if necessary

3. Embed the chart from the worksheet beneath the spreadsheet extract in the document and resize it if necessary.

4. Save the document as **Regional Sales** and close it.

5. Open **Sales** in *Excel*.

6. On the **Sales** sheet, change the figure for **Central** in **June** to **£150,000**.

7. Save the file and close *Excel*.

8. Open the document **Regional Sales** and update the links. Notice the chart doesn't change.

9. Break the link to **Sales.xlsx**.

10. Save and close the **Regional Sales** document.

If you experienced any difficulty completing this Revision refer back to the Driving Lessons in this section. Then redo the Revision.

Once you are confident with the features, complete the Record of Achievement Matrix referring to the section at the end of the guide. Only when competent move on to the next Section.

Section 13
Macros

By the end of this Section you should be able to

Record a Macro

Run a Macro

Assign a Macro to a Button

To gain an understanding of the above features, work through the **Driving Lessons** in this **Section**.

For each **Driving Lesson**, read the **Park and Read** instructions, without touching the keyboard, then work through the numbered steps of the **Manoeuvres** on the computer. Complete the **Revision Exercise(s)** at the end of the section to test your knowledge.

Driving Lesson 76 - Recording a Macro

🅿 Park and Read

A **Macro** records keystrokes and menu selections, then plays them back exactly as they were recorded. The use of macros results in the more efficient production of documents. Once macros have been created, they can be used at any time in any document that uses the same template.

A new macro can be created easily, but great care must be taken during the recording, because each action taken is incorporated into the macro.

Manoeuvres

1. Create a new document, select the **Developer** tab and click ⌐ Record Macro.

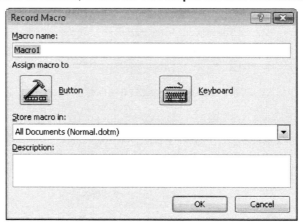

*Storing the macro in the **Normal** template means it will be available to in all documents. It is also possible to store macros with the current document only.*

2. Enter the **Macro name** as **Landscape** and in Description, enter **Change page setup** to replace the text.

3. Click **OK**. At this point ▣ is displayed in the **Status Bar** and the mouse pointer has changed to a cassette tape, showing that the macro will now record all actions performed.

While recording a macro the mouse cannot be used at certain times, for example, when moving the insertion point around within the document or selecting text, the keyboard must be used.

4. Select the **Page Layout** tab. From **Orientation** select **Landscape**.

Driving Lesson 76 - Continued

5.   Select the **Stop Recording** button, ◾, to end the recording.

6.   Close the document <u>without</u> saving.

7.   A second macro will add fields to the headers and footers. Start a new document.

8.   Select to **Record Macro**. Name the macro **Footer** and click **OK**.

9.   From the **Insert** tab select **Header** and then **Edit Header**.

10.   From the **Insert** group, click on **Quick Parts** and then **Field**. At the **Field** dialog box, from **Categories** select **Document Information**.

11.   From **Field names** select **FileName** and then **OK**. Click on **Go to Footer**.

12.   At the cursor position, type in your name, the press **<Tab>** twice to move to the right of the footer.

13.   From the **Insert** group, insert the **Date**.

14.   Close the **Header and Footer** and **Stop** the macro. Close the document without saving.

15.   A third macro will create a table that will repeat its header row over several pages. Start a new document.

16.   Start a new macro called **TableHeader**. Use the **Insert** tab to insert a **Table** and using the default setting, i.e. 5 columns and 2 rows. Enter **Monday**, **Tuesday**, **Wednesday**, etc., across the first row.

17.   Select the first row using the **Layout** tab, then Select and **Select Row**. Centre and embolden the text.

ℹ️   *In macro mode certain selections cannot be made via the mouse.*

18.   Return to the **Layout** tab and from the **Data** group, select the option to **Repeat Header Rows**.

19.   Launch the **Table Properties** dialog box.

20.   From the **Row** tab click **Next Row**. In **Size** for Row 2, **Specify** a row height of **5 cm**, then **Stop** recording the macro.

21.   From the **Developer** tab, click on **Macros**, to review the created macros.

22.   **Cancel** the dialog box and close all documents <u>without</u> saving.

Driving Lesson 77 - Running a Macro

Park and Read

Once a macro has been created and recorded, it can be run at any time.

Manoeuvres

1.   Open the document **Summary**.

2.   From the **Developer** tab select **Macros**.

3.   From **Macros in**, select **All active templates and documents** and **Landscape** from the list.

4.   Click **Run** to run the macro.

5.   Print the document.

6.   Close the document <u>without</u> saving.

7.   Open the document **Discovery**.

8.   Select **Macros** and run the **Footer** macro.

9.   **Print Preview** the document to ensure that the macro has used the correct information.

10. Close the document without saving.

Driving Lesson 78 - Assigning a Macro to a Button

▣ Park and Read

The **Customize** dialog box can be used to assign a macro to a button on a toolbar. The button can then be added to any toolbar. The appearance of the button can also be changed. This can be done before or after the macro is recorded.

☞ Manoeuvres

1. Start a new document and select the **Office Button** and **Word Options**. Click on **Customize**.

2. From **Choose commands from**, scroll down the list of **Categories** until **Macros** appears.

3. Click on **Macros** to view all the macros created.

4. Click on **Normal.NewMacros.TableHeader**. Click on **Add** to add it to the **Quick Access Toolbar**.

5. Click on **Modify** and in the **Display name** box enter **Table**.

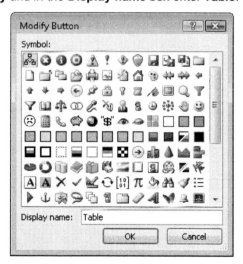

6. Select the smiley face from the buttons.

7. Click **OK** twice to return to *Word*.

8. Run the macro by clicking the button.

Driving Lesson 78 - Continued

9.   To see the table header at work, press **<Tab>** until the table is large enough to cover two pages. Check that the header row is repeated.

10.   Remove the button from the toolbar by right clicking on it and selecting **Remove from Quick Access Toolbar**.

11.   To delete the macro, select **Macros**.

12.   Select the **TableHeader** macro, then click **Delete**.

13.   Select **Yes** at the prompt.

14.   Delete the remaining macros and click **Close**.

15.   Close the document <u>without</u> saving.

Driving Lesson 79 - Revision: Macros

This is not an ECDL test. Testing may only be carried out through certified ECDL test centres. This covers the features introduced in this section. Try not to refer to the preceding Driving Lessons while completing it.

1. Open the document **Stately Home**.

2. Create a new macro to print the current page of a document.

3. Name the macro **Page**.

4. Move to page 2 and run the **Page** macro.

5. Assign the macro to a button on the **Quick Access Toolbar**. Select the **eye** button.

6. Move to page 3 and run the macro using the new button.

7. Remove the button from the toolbar.

8. Delete the macro.

9. Close the document <u>without</u> saving.

If you experienced any difficulty completing this Revision refer back to the Driving Lessons in this section. Then redo the Revision.

Once you are confident with the features, complete the Record of Achievement Matrix referring to the section at the end of the guide.

Answers

Driving Lesson 5

Step 1   Purpose and audience.

Step 2   Spreadsheets, database tables for merge, images from libraries.

Step 3   Master document.

Step 4   Templates.

Step 5   Hyperlinks.

Step 6   **.txt** format.

Step 7   Web page.

Driving Lesson 12

Step 7   Simply use the **Paste** button.

Driving Lesson 14

Step 7   Only a single line is left at the top of the page. This is a widow.

Driving Lesson 32

Step 9   S Westgarth is last on the list.

Driving Lesson 50

Step 10   **Original Showing Markup.**

Glossary

AutoText	A tool that inserts pre-stored phrases or graphics to text, avoiding repetitive keyboard entries.
Bookmark	A named location or selection of text, which can then be used for reference purposes or searching.
Caption	A numbered label that can be added to various types of object within a document. The numbering can be automatic.
Comment	A note added to a specific location or selected text within a document that is displayed as a **ScreenTip** above the associated text.
Cross-reference	Used to refer to an item elsewhere in a document.
Data Source	A file containing records, that can be merged with a main document. This file may be a document, database or spreadsheet.
Endnote	A piece of text that is placed at the end of a document, giving further information about a text entry or object within it. Numbers are automatically placed within the document, next to the text to be referenced and the note text.
Field	A placeholder within a document that contains a field code, which inserts current information, e.g. page number, date, etc.
Field Code	The instructions within a field that generate the information to be inserted.
Footnote	A piece of text that is placed at the foot of a page, giving further information about a text entry or object on that page. Numbers are automatically placed within the document, next to the text to be referenced and the note text.
Indent	A measurement by which text is moved away from either the left or right margin.
Justified	An alignment setting that provides straight margins at both left and right.
Mail Merge	A facility that combines a main document with records held within a data source.
Main Document	A document containing merge fields, where information from a data source is to be inserted.

Master Document	A document that is made up of a number of separate files or sub-documents.
Object	An item imported or created, e.g. picture, drawing, chart.
Orphan	The first line of a paragraph that is separated from the rest and left at the bottom of the current page.
Outline	A view of the document that displays the hierarchy of styles used within it.
Password to Modify	A level of protection that allows a document to be opened and altered, but modifications can only be saved if a new file name is used.
ScreenTip	Notes that appear in yellow boxes, giving extra information about specific text or objects within a document. They are usually displayed when the cursor is positioned or clicked over the appropriate location.
Section	Part of a document that is to be formatted differently from the rest e.g. page numbering or layout. Created by section breaks.
Style	Pre-created combinations of formatting, consisting of paragraph and font formats.
Sub-document	A document that is a component part of a master document. Sub-documents may be opened and edited individually, but remain linked to the master document.
Template	A base document that contains elements of formatting and alignment and that can be used over and over again.
Text Orientation	The formatting that determines whether text reads horizontally or vertically on the page.
Text Wrapping	The formatting that determines how text flows (wraps) around inserted objects such as graphics.
Tracking	A feature that makes it possible to see where and when changes were made to a document and who made them.
Watermark	An object (which may be a text box) that is placed on the background of a page, so that text appears over the top of it.
Widow	The final line of a paragraph that is separated from the rest and printed at the top of a new page.
WordArt	A graphical text feature. **WordArt** is manipulated in the same way as other objects.

Index

Record of Achievement Matrix

This Matrix is to be used to measure your progress while working through the guide. This is a learning reinforcement process, you judge when you are competent.

Tick boxes are provided for each feature. 1 is for no knowledge, 2 some knowledge and 3 is for competent. A section is only complete when column 3 is completed for all parts of the section.

For details on sitting ECDL Examinations in your country please contact the local ECDL Licensee or visit the European Computer Driving Licence Foundation Limited web site at http://www.ecdl.org.

Tick the Relevant Boxes **1**: No Knowledge **2**: Some Knowledge **3**: Competent

Section	No.	Driving Lesson	1	2	3
1 Working Efficiently	1	Design			
	2	Techniques			
	3	Hyperlinks			
	4	Saving			
2 Text Editing	6	Find and Replace			
	7	Paste Special Options			
	8	AutoCorrect			
	9	AutoFormat			
	10	AutoText			
	11	Text Flow and Wrap			
3 Paragraph Editing	13	Line Spacing			
	14	Pagination Options			
	15	Creating Styles			
	16	Modifying Styles			
	17	Outline Level Styles			
	18	Multilevel Lists			
4 Document Setup	20	Adding/Deleting Section Breaks			
	21	Applying Section Formatting			
	22	Section Headers and Footers			
	23	Multiple Column Layout			
	24	Modifying Column Layout			
	25	Modifying Column Width/Spacing			
	26	Creating a Watermark			
	27	Modifying and Deleting Watermarks			
5 Tables	29	Table Styles			
	30	Merging a Splitting Cells			
	31	Converting Text to Table			
	32	Sorting Table Data			
	33	Performing Calculations			
	34	Table Properties and Setup			

Tick the Relevant Boxes **1**: No Knowledge   **2**: Some Knowledge   **3**: Competent

Section	No.	Driving Lesson	1	2	3
6 Referencing	36	Creating Footnotes and Endnotes			
	37	Modifying/Deleting Footnotes/Endnotes			
	38	Creating a Table of Contents			
	39	Updating a Table of Contents			
	40	Adding and Deleting Bookmarks			
	41	Cross-Referencing			
	42	Adding Numbered Captions			
	43	Creating a Table of Figures			
	44	Creating an Index			
7 Collaborative Editing	46	Adding/Editing Comments			
	47	Tracking Changes			
	48	Accept/Rejecting Changes			
	49	Compare and Combine			
8 Document Security	51	Password Protection			
	52	Removing/Changing Passwords			
9 Master Documents and Templates	54	Creating a Master Document			
	55	Creating a Subdocument			
	56	Adding/Removing Subdocument			
	57	Modifying a Template			
10 Field Codes and Forms	59	Working with Field Codes			
	60	Editing and Updating Field Codes			
	61	Locking/Unlocking Fields			
	62	Creating and Editing Forms			
	63	Form Field Options			
	64	Protecting Form Fields			
11 Mail Merge	66	Editing a Data Source			
	67	Sorting a Data Source			
	68	Using Different Data Sources			
	69	ASK and IF Fields			
12 Linking and Embedding	71	Linking Data			
	72	Updating Links			
	73	Embedding Data			
	74	Modifying Embedded Data			
13 Macros	76	Recording a Macro			
	77	Running a Macro			
	78	Assigning a Macro to a Button			

Other Products from CiA Training Ltd

CiA Training Ltd is a leading publishing company, which has consistently delivered the highest quality products since 1985. A wide range of flexible and easy to use self teach resources has been developed by CiA's experienced publishing team to aid the learning process. These include the following ECDL Foundation approved products at the time of publication of this product:

- **ECDL/ICDL Syllabus 5.0**

- **ECDL/ICDL Advanced Syllabus 2.0**

- **ECDL/ICDL Revision Series**

- **ECDL/ICDL Advanced Syllabus 2.0 Revision Series**

- **e-Citizen**

Previous syllabus versions also available - contact us for further details.

We hope you have enjoyed using our materials and would love to hear your opinions about them. If you'd like to give us some feedback, please go to:

www.ciatraining.co.uk/feedback.php

and let us know what you think.

New products are constantly being developed. For up to the minute information on our products, to view our full range, to find out more, or to be added to our mailing list, visit:

www.ciatraining.co.uk